A HISTORY OF
WORSHIP IN THE CHURCH
OF SCOTLAND

by

WILLIAM D. MAXWELL
T.D., Ph.D., D.D.

Minister at Whitekirk and Tyninghame

GEOFFREY CUMBERLEGE

OXFORD UNIVERSITY PRESS

LONDON   GLASGOW   NEW YORK

1955

Oxford University Press, Amen House, London E.C.4

GLASGOW NEW YORK TORONTO MELBOURNE WELLINGTON
BOMBAY CALCUTTA MADRAS KARACHI CAPE TOWN IBADAN

Geoffrey Cumberlege, Publisher to the University

Printed in Great Britain by
The Camelot Press Ltd., London and Southampton

J. Golder McGregor
with best wishes
from
James Ferguson

Christmas, 1955.

A HISTORY OF
WORSHIP IN THE CHURCH
OF SCOTLAND

THE BAIRD LECTURES 1953

Preface

I RECORD at once my thanks to the Trustees of the Baird Trust for appointing me their lecturer for the years 1952-3 and for the confidence they reposed in me.

To give in six lectures a just and balanced account of the forms of worship used at the principal service on Sundays in the Church of Scotland from earliest times to the present day is not easy to accomplish. All details cannot be included, but what is should be representative and typical, and the facts presented in their true proportion. This I have tried to do, acknowledging also in the footnotes my debt to those who have preceded me in this field of studies.

For present help of scrutiny and advice I am indebted to many friends. I express my thanks also to the Principal and the staff of New College, Edinburgh, for their hospitality, and to the Librarian for his tolerance and patience.

W. D. M.

MANSE OF WHITEKIRK,
DUNBAR, EAST LOTHIAN,
December 1954

Acknowledgement

Acknowledgement is made to the S.P.C.K. and the Church Union for permission to include the quotations from *Liturgy and Worship*, edited by W. K. Lowther Clarke, appearing on pp. 10 and 39-40.

Contents

I

The Early Worship of
Celts and Scots

ALTHOUGH during the later period of the Roman
occupation of Britain evidence exists that Christians
were to be found in the land we now call Scotland,
and especially in that part of the country lying north of
Carlisle and the Tweed and south of the Clyde and the
Forth, it was St. Ninian who in the early part of the fifth
century knit Christians together into an organized life,[1]
and by his apostolic labours not only increased their
numbers but consolidated the faith among them, and
laid a sure foundation upon which others might build.
It is true that there were relapses and changes, and the
records are far from continuous; yet from Ninian springs
not only the monastically organized Christianity of Scotland,[2] but also to a large extent that of Ireland which
nurtured St. Columba and a noble company of Irish and
Celtic saints and missioners. His work has been described
by others; he interests us here because through him we
may perhaps catch a glimpse of what the first worship
in Scotland among Christians was like, indigenous records
of which there are none.

Extensive and precise details of St. Ninian's life and
work elude us, but certain basic facts look as if they

[1] Dowden, *Celtic Church*, p. 27; and Dr. Douglas Simpson's invaluable
studies, *The Celtic Church in Scotland* (Aberdeen, 1935) and *St. Ninian*
(Aberdeen, 1944); and Hutchison Cockburn, *The Celtic Church in Dunblane*
(1954).
[2] I use Scotland and Ireland in their modern sense throughout.

might reasonably be accepted.[1] He was born in the last quarter of the fourth century of royal and Christian parents in Galloway, and completed his education by studying for several years at Rome.[2] He was then, it may be, consecrated bishop by the Pope, and returned as a missionary to his own country about the year 397. On the way home, he visited the aged and famous St. Martin of Tours. Thus, out of what he had learned at Rome and at Tours, he found a model for his work in Scotland; and was fortunate in being able to do that work during a comparatively peaceful period.[3]

Therefore, if we can determine the form of worship used at Rome at the end of the fourth century, we have modest grounds for supposing that Ninian followed it closely when he returned to Scotland; for, as Bede tells us, Ninian was 'regularly' instructed at Rome in both the Christian faith and mysteries. That is to say, he received instruction there not only in theology, but also in worship and the sacraments. And, as Dr. Douglas Simpson[4] rightly reminds us, 'The monastic settlement established by St. Ninian at Whithorn was an expansion of the contemporary Christianity of the Roman Empire; and we must beware of conceiving it to have displayed the peculiar characteristics which the Celtic Church afterwards developed in Britain and Ireland, at a time when the

[1] The controversy about St. Ninian still continues among scholars. The latest but not the last word has been said in the volumes of the Dumfriesshire and Galloway Natural History and Antiquarian Society, vols. XXVII and XXX (1948-9 and 1951-2) of the Third Series of their *Transactions*. The footnotes of the papers in these volumes mention the chief writers and their works—Black, Levison, Douglas Simpson, and others. What I offer above, therefore, must be treated as possible (or probable) rather than established fact. My own opinion is that the weight of evidence is still on the side of Dr. Douglas Simpson, especially in so far as the earlier life of Ninian and his labours in the south of Scotland are described by him.

[2] 'Rome' and 'Roman' in these lectures refer to the city itself, and are used in the local and not in the modern denominational sense.

[3] Cf., e.g., Collingwood, *Roman Britain*, pp. 288, 310, etc.

[4] *The Celtic Church in Scotland*, pp. 50-51.

"barbarian" invasions had cut it off from the Empire'.

What then was Christian worship like in Rome at this time?[1] It was, judged both by later and by Eastern standards, extremely simple and compact, and terse and restrained in its expression and ceremonial. Also, very shortly before this the Roman rite had been translated from Greek into Latin, the native tongue, and was passing through a lively formative period, influenced by St. Ambrose in the shaping of the liturgy and in evangelical and musical reforms. For it may now be considered as almost beyond doubt that St. Ambrose was the real pioneer in this liturgical movement in Rome under Pope Damasus (366-84), though Ambrose himself in his *De Sacramentis* says that he followed at Milan 'the type and form of the great church at Rome in all things', reserving the right to make slight changes to meet special local circumstances, and to eliminate Arian innovations of his predecessor. The worship at Rome (and Milan) conformed to the structure common to all Christian worship, falling into the two main parts, the liturgy of the catechumens and the liturgy of the faithful, derived respectively from the synagogue and the upper room.[2]

[1] See E. Bishop, *Liturgica Historica*, essay on 'The Genius of the Roman Rite'. The description given on the following pages is of a solemn celebration by the Pope, and is therefore more elaborate and attended by a greater number of clergy than an ordinary celebration would have been. Yet it is essentially simple, compared with later developments.

[2] See my *Outline of Christian Worship* for expansion and application of this statement. O. Cullman in his *Le Culte dans l'Eglise primitive* discards, I think rashly, the view that the liturgy of the catechumens derives from the synagogue. Certainly many elements in it were not taken directly from the worship of the synagogue, but no one suggests that the derivation of every detail is particular and precise; Christian worship quickly developed in conformity with the new spirit, but the general influence and background of the synagogue were inevitably strong factors in its form and first moulding (see, e.g., Oesterley, *Jewish Background of the Christian Liturgy*). The worship of the Temple also influenced Christian worship, but of necessity in doctrine rather than detail of ritual or ceremonial, and particularly in the doctrine of sacrifice (see, as a brilliant introductory essay, F. C. N. Hicks in *Ways of Worship* (London, 1952), pp. 204 sqq.).

Before the service began, the singers gathered in their places and sang a psalm with antiphon and concluding (as did all psalms) with a doxology, to a simple plainsong chant from side to side. This psalm derived its name 'introit' from the fact that while it was being sung, the celebrant entered attended by his assisting or concelebrating ministers who walked two-by-two. Bending low in a brief private prayer he took his position standing[1] behind the holy table, reverently kissing it, his ministers about him and the deacons standing at each end of the holy table. The celebrant faced the people and the east, for the orientation at least of the Constantinian basilicas was opposite to what is now general.[2] The psalm being concluded upon a sign from the celebrant, he greeted the people, saying, 'The Lord be with you', to which they replied, 'And with thy spirit'; whereupon he called them to prayer and said a short collect, a terse form of prayer uniquely Roman in character and locus.

He then retired to his great chair in the apse while from a low pulpit assisting ministers read passages from the Bible which culminated invariably in a reading from a Gospel. Between the readings, usually just before the gospel,[3] another psalm (an integral part of the liturgy) was sung, known as the 'gradual' because the leading singer or singers sang from the 'gradus' or step of a pulpit or ambo the choir answering with a refrain from

[1] From earliest times the celebrant at the holy table always stood and never knelt when he was leading the solemn action of the eucharist. When not specifically engaged in the action, he sat in his great chair behind the table (later in a sedilium laterally placed), and often, following Jewish custom or the emperor upon his throne, he preached while sitting in his chair. The people also generally stood for prayer, kneeling being a later innovation.

[2] J. G. Davies, *Origin and Development of Early Christian Church Architecture* (London, 1952), p. 81.

[3] If there were three readings, it may be that the gradual followed the prophecy and the 'alleluia' the epistle (see Cabrol, *The Mass of the Western Rites*, p. 55, and *Liturgia*, p. 520).

the same psalm. At the reading of the gospel, a moving and deeply evangelical ceremony emphasized its centrality: the gospel-book was carried from the holy table with lights and incense to the high ambo at the south side of the church—that is, on the celebrant's right—where, facing the north, a deacon sang the gospel as a proclamation[1] of Christ the King at which the people stood. Now that the orientation of churches is generally opposite to that of the church we are describing, in present Roman usage the deacon, obeying the old rubric, finds himself at the north side of the sanctuary facing north, and facing therefore the wall of the church instead of standing on the south side facing partly towards the people as the rubric originally intended.

After the gospel, the celebrant from his great chair preached the sermon, and then called the people to prayer, saying 'Let us pray'. Whether by the fifth century this prayer of the faithful had disappeared at Rome, it is difficult to say; it still existed in North Africa in St. Augustine's time, and one apparent instance of it remains in the Roman missal today in the mass of the Presanctified on Good Friday.[2] It consists of a series of collects of

[1] It is to be noted that the Church has always regarded the reading of the Holy Scriptures (and especially the gospel) as a proclamation from God the Most High, and not as a 'reading together'. We find the same attitude to Holy Scripture in Jewish worship; it is exemplified in the 'Shemah' ('Hear, O Israel . . .') and constant in the prophetic books. Similarly in the Church of Scotland the reading of the Bible is traditionally introduced by the words 'Hear the Word of God', &c. People may properly and usefully be encouraged to follow in their own Bibles the readings from Holy Scripture, but the sense of proclamation, of 'a Word of God' declared unto men should never be obscured or lost by private or sentimental revision of this Scriptural formula. The seemly and rewarding custom of standing for the reading of the gospel is now being revived in some Scottish churches, bringing with it a new sense of urgency and authority to the Scriptures and of the presence of the living Lord speaking through His Word.

[2] On the other hand, the prayer now missing after this bidding 'Oremus', may have been a prayer 'super sidonem', said when the white linen cloth was spread upon the altar, and would thus have been the first prayer of the liturgy of the faithful.

intercession said by the celebrant. Before each collect he bids the people to pray specifically for the subject of the intercession, and the deacon calls upon the people to kneel for a brief moment of silent prayer, then to rise up, after which the celebrant says the collect. This concluded the first part of the service, the core of which is the reading and exposition of the Holy Scriptures.

The second part of the service, the liturgy of the faithful, began with the collection of the gifts of bread and wine and their preparation for consecration. Two deacons spread the white linen cloth upon the holy table, covering the top or 'mensa', while the celebrant with deacons went down to the tables of prothesis[1] to receive the people's gifts, carried them back to the altar, where the deacons prepared such as were to be used for the holy mystery. While all this, which corresponded to our Lord's action when 'he took bread . . . and the cup', was proceeding, the 'schola' or choir sang another psalm now known as the offertory; and meantime the celebrant went to his seat behind the holy table, and there washed his hands before handling holy things, saying 'I will wash my hands in innocency' (Ps. 26.6).

Thereafter, he returned to the altar to begin the consecration, corresponding to our Lord's action when 'he gave thanks and blessed'. Standing at the west side of the holy table, he faced east with his presbyters grouped around him standing with their heads deeply bowed; while the deacons went to the east side of the holy table, standing erect and facing the celebrant, to lead the responses of the people, which consisted of the 'Amen's', the replies to the salutation, the 'Lift up your hearts', and

---

[1] See J. G. Davies, op. cit., p. 47. Tables of prothesis, or one table only, were set in either the sanctuary or the nave to receive the people's gifts of bread and wine, and to prepare them for the holy mystery. They survive still in the East for the preparation of the elements, and in the West are now either niches in the wall or credence tables.

the hymn of the cherubim, 'Holy, Holy, Holy'. First, the celebrant said the secret (i.e., silent) collect, and raised his voice at the conclusion. Then he went on to the salutation and 'Lift up your hearts', and so to the consecration. Standing, with hands extended in the ancient attitude of solemn prayer, he sang the preface or great thanksgiving which concluded with the singing of the 'Holy, Holy, Holy' in which all joined, bending low with the celebrant. Then the celebrant, standing erect while all the people bent low, said the remainder of the prayer in a solemn spoken tone, a prayer very similar, if not precisely in all respects, to the present Roman canon.[1] Or, if his ministers (presbyters) concelebrated with him, they joined him in singing the preface and reciting the canon. At the conclusion of this great prayer, he gave the kiss of peace to his ministers, and through them to the people.

Then, following the action of our Lord when 'he brake the bread', the celebrant performed the fraction, i.e., the breaking of the bread and its attendant ceremonies; and afterwards said the Lord's Prayer, with an embolism, a short added prayer which is an enlargement of the 'Deliver us from evil'.

The celebrant now, in obedience to our Lord's action when 'he gave', and setting the example, received communion in both kinds at the hands of a deacon and then gave to his ministers, who in turn communicated the people who came forward to stand at the holy table to receive. Meanwhile the choir sang another psalm, 'O taste and see' (34.8), now known as the 'communion', and the celebrant sat in his chair while the action proceeded.

When all had received in both kinds, the celebrant returned to the altar, greeted the people, and said a short collect. A deacon then dismissed the people saying

[1] See, e.g., Cabrol, *Mass of the Western Rites*, pp. 39 sqq.

B

'Ite missa est',[1] and they replied 'Thanks be to God', and the clergy in procession retired from the church.

Although it takes some time to describe this service, it was simple and short in all its essentials. The collect was a strict form of brief direct prayer, and the prayer of consecration was itself brief compared with the contemporary liturgies of the East and the later Gallican liturgies. The ceremonial too was simple and central, and the whole service probably extended over less than two hours, which was indeed short judged by the general standards of the time. Throughout we see the Roman genius for brevity, centrality, and simple directness almost to the point of bluntness.

A word too must be said about the setting of the service, the building in which it took place,[2] for such buildings still stand in Rome. It was a basilica, not large, primarily a rectangular building with a barrel roof. At the west end was a platform raised by several steps mounting to it on the north and south sides; this formed the sanctuary which extended into a semicircular apse. At the extreme west end stood the bishop's chair, with seats or benches for his presbyters. Forward of this, under the great arch where the apse joined the rectangular building, or even farther forward if the raised sanctuary floor extended boldly beyond the arch,[3] stood the holy table surrounded by four pillars which supported a veil or canopy (ciborium) above it and from which lights were hung. The

---

[1] The word by which this service came to be commonly known in the West was 'mass', derived from 'missa' which simply meant 'dismissal'. Originally it had no doctrinal significance, as indeed strictly speaking it still has none.

[2] See J. G. Davies's invaluable study, mentioned above.

[3] The modern tendency to set the holy table within the apse instead of beneath the great arch, and to cut off the sanctuary floor at the arch by beginning the steps there, is to be discouraged because it produces a cramped and crowded effect in the sanctuary itself, restricts the space required for the movement of clergy and elders, removes the holy table from the people, and destroys that sense of spaciousness which gives character and dignity to God's House.

sanctuary was divided from the rest of the church by a low partition, the 'cancellus'.

Symbolical of the presence of the great company of the faithful, the heavenly church was portrayed in mosaic or fresco: along the walls of the nave above the heads of the people were saints, martyrs, and confessors; and higher still were the apostles and a procession of angels carrying the instruments of the mysteries.[1] In the apse, and seeming to hover over the holy table, the ascended Lord was depicted, victorious, interceding, and seated in glory in the midst of the angelic orders. At the east end of the nave the circle was closed, often by an empty throne, before which creation stands waiting for the rising of the Sun of Righteousness at the last judgement.

It was such worship in such a building that St. Ninian saw and shared at Rome, and it must have made a profound impression upon him. It is undoubted that he would bring it in its essentials to Britain. Necessarily, it would at first be shorn of much of its splendour in setting and ceremonial, for fewer clergy would be available, and churches inevitably cruder and barer would have to be built and music taught. But it will be noticed that he set about this at once, when he built the first stone church at Whithorn and established his monks on the Isle with their school of boys to whom they taught singing, letters, and agriculture.[2] Ninian himself, and his disciples, wherever they went in England, Scotland, and Ireland, appear to have set up similar centres upon the three-fold pattern of St. Martin of Tours, namely, a cell for the abbot, and standing apart from this a small monastery for monks

[1] 'Just as the Saviour is where two or three are gathered in his name, so also are present, invisible like him but like him present, all those who are joined with him beyond the veil and can no longer be separated from him.' Bouyer, The Paschal Mystery, p. 55.

[2] Douglas Simpson, St. Ninian.

with a school, and again at a distance away a church
was built for worship.

Of this worship in the early Ninianic churches we have
no contemporary records; but when records do emerge
we find the services based upon the fundamental order
and structure described, but more elaborate and exotic.
This elaboration occurred not only in Scotland and Ireland, but universally beyond Rome among those peoples
who did not possess the disciplined sense of order and
simplicity characteristic of the Roman genius. Later,
some of these elaborations were adopted at Rome after
the incursions of the barbarians, but they did not originate
there. Gavin describes the process clearly and briefly:

The complex history of the Roman liturgy makes it difficult to trace with the same definiteness we can use of the
oriental liturgies. . . . Liturgical variation was much freer
in the west and 'free liturgical composition prevailed in the
west up into the Merovingian period. . . . The ideal seems
at times to be to supply for each feast day its own liturgy.
This effort, while not entirely suppressed, confined itself in
Rome to the formulation of an unvarying fixed kernel of
prayers of which the core was the consecration. But exactly
when this canon of the mass was stabilized we do not know.
Its present form dates from the sixth century. Careful examination of the text shows that its basis was the ancient Hippo-
lytan liturgy.'[1] In the Carolingian period the two groups of
Western liturgies—Ambrosian, Mozarabic, and Gallican, and
the Roman—influenced each other. Ambrosian ideas came
over into the Roman, while Roman usages and prayers were
injected into the Gallican. . . . The mixed Roman-Carolingian
liturgy in its conflated form was to become normative in
the west.[2]

The first liturgy of which the text has come down to

[1] Lietzmann, *Messe und Herrenmahl*, p. 262.
[2] In *Liturgy and Worship*, pp. 120-1; see also Bishop, *Liturgica Historica*,
and Cabrol, *Western Rites*.

us reflecting Celtic usage is that contained in the famous Stowe Missal,[1] dating from the eighth to the tenth centuries, but it is generally agreed reflecting earlier practices. This leaves a gap of three or four centuries—in Scotland and Ireland an unsettled and largely unknown period—and many changes no doubt took place; yet as the Stowe Missal shows, the earlier pattern persisted though in a more elaborate form. We are not to suppose, however, that worship was the same in all its details everywhere throughout Scotland and Ireland. The time had not come when men thought in terms of set uniformity—though they were always faithful to the underlying structure of the liturgy—and the western rites differed greatly from each other in every part of Europe, and even local rites often varied from Sunday to Sunday and certainly from feast to feast. The Stowe Missal itself represents no more than a local use, even if the 'locus' may have been large. Furthermore, during the eighth and ninth centuries, and later, the monkish missionaries travelled widely, penetrating into the Low Countries, and along the Rhine and Danube, that great trade route with the East, up which as well as through Marseilles and Lyons must have come many eastern influences and practices which were adopted in Gallican and Celtic rites—not to speak of the eastern influences active in Italy and Spain.

Many customs and innovations were exchanged and collected, beloved of the Celts whose warm romanticism and love of symbol also created new rites and ceremonies.

---

[1] The Henry Bradshaw Society has edited this missal: and it has been edited and translated, together with Roman, Ambrosian, Gallican, Mozarabic, and other western rites by West in his *Western Liturgies*. A useful compendium of Celtic liturgical and devotional documents is given in L. Gougaud, *Christianity in Celtic Lands,* pp. 313 sqq., and in Cabrol, op. cit. For specifically Scottish documents, &c., together with a brief description and where they are to be found, see D. McRoberts, *Catalogue of Scottish Medieval Liturgical Books and Fragments.*

Warren,[1] apparently with approval, quotes Mabillon:
'the Irish differed from the ritual and rule of other
churches and celebrated the holy eucharist with great
variation and multiplication of prayers.' This is a most
misleading statement; in the continental Gallican rites
great multiplicity and variety of prayers is to be found,
even in the prayer of consecration itself where the content varied enormously,[2] but the basic structure was
retained. The Irish and the Scots did not at all differ
from the ritual and rule of a great many other Churches
of this period in celebrating 'the holy eucharist with great
variation and multiplication of prayers'.

We see, too, from the clashes between the Celtic and
English Churches during this period, that there were
many differences between them. These differences fall
into two classes: first, the old Roman customs still maintained among the Celts which by Augustine of Canterbury's time had been abandoned by Rome itself. The
Easter controversy is an example of this: the Celts still
used the old Roman calendar which shortly after Ninian's
time was altered in Rome, and Augustine who came to
England later was naturally one of those who used the
new calendar: but both calendars came from Rome.

The pagan calendar, together with the pagan cults,
was finally abolished and the Christian calendar enforced
by the Emperor Theodosius,[3] and this reform was still
in progress when Ninian came to Rome. As Cochrane in
his *Christianity and Classical Culture* points out, 'To Theodosius the European world owes the existence of a uni-
form calendar corresponding to the needs of a universal
society and based upon the Christian year.'[4] Thus the
calendar used by the Celts represented the final triumph

[1] *Celtic Rite*, p. 96.
[2] See, e.g., the texts in Neale and Forbes, *Gallican Liturgies*.
[3] *Cod. Theod.*, ii, *De Feriis*.   [4] p. 330.

over paganism in the western world, and was the more precious to them on that account. Accordingly, as Warren[1] states, originally 'the practice of the British harmonized with that of the Roman Church, the most ancient Roman table for Easter agreeing with that of the British Church; but . . . the Celtic Church had never adopted the various alterations and improvements which on astronomical . . . grounds had been from time to time accepted by the Continental Church'.

The second class of differences were those that grew up in Celtic usage either spontaneously or by importation from Gaul, Saxony, or elsewhere.

There is not much, however, to be gained by tabulating all these differences, as Warren and others have attempted to do, and it may even prove to be misleading. Where they came from, how they got there, and who brought them, cannot now be accurately determined. In any event, they can prove nothing more than what is stated above, and nearly all of them can be found in the Gallican rites in one form or another. Further, because of the paucity of the Scots and Celtic rites that have come down to us, it is impossible to have any complete and certain knowledge of all the varieties of rites and ceremonies used in Scotland. It is an interesting but scarcely ultimately rewarding study for those fond of the curious; but it is idle to attempt to deduce very much from what we find, and especially to attempt to support the old fable, as baseless as the legend that St. Andrew landed upon the coast of Fife, that the Celtic rites derived from a *direct and primitive* connexion with the East.

We are also to keep in mind that what we know as high or sung mass[2] was everywhere the norm in the West, and whatever alterations took place were to this service.

---

[1] op. cit., p. 64. Warren wrongly dates the change as from Nicæa.
[2] Cf. Warren, op. cit., p. 125.

Low mass, the later popular service spoken rapidly in an undertone without any singing, was barely known at this period. Also, in Scotland and Ireland celebrations, in accord with early custom, were weekly, not daily, and on saints' days.[1] It is interesting, too, to find that concelebration, common at Rome in Ninian's day, was favoured by the Celtic Church for centuries after it had practically disappeared elsewhere. But the Celtic method of concelebration differed soon if not always from the Roman method. At Rome the bishop concelebrated with his presbyters; in Scotland and Ireland the bishop appears always to have celebrated alone, but it was common for two or more presbyters to concelebrate when a bishop was not present or taking part.[2]

Cabrol has summed the matter up thus:

Everyone knows that the Celts of Ireland and England [and Scotland] were the most daring travellers at the beginning of the middle ages. They left their mark on all the countries of Europe.[3] The greater part of these missionaries were monks who carried liturgical MSS. in their wallets; many among them were cultivated men and good copyists, and their books are found in the oldest libraries. The researches of those who have in our own days made a study of Celtic influences show that such influences were more extensive than they had at one time been held to be. To begin with, it seems that there never has been a Celtic liturgy in the ordinary sense; to use this expression then is apt to lead to confusion, as if there had been in Celtic countries an autonomous liturgy, or even a liturgy with special characteristics, like the latin liturgies we have just been treating of [i.e., Roman, Ambrosian, Mozarabic, and Gallican]. It happens that the Celts, who were great travellers and ardent lovers

[1] Warren, op. cit., pp. 140 sq. For days and times of celebrations in the early Church see A. McArthur's scholarly study, *The Evolution of the Christian Year*.

[2] Warren, op. cit., pp. 128 sqq.

[3] See, e.g., W. Levison, *England and the Continent in the Eighth Century*.

of the liturgy, were also indefatigable in collecting every book of the kind, in copying and retouching them, and sometimes adding a formula here and a rite there of their own invention. . . . Only in the domain of private prayer [and he should have added 'of hymnody'] does Celtic originality appear, and there Celtic piety has free course.[1]

It is therefore impossible to describe Celtic worship exactly; its ceremonial, words, and music must have varied considerably in different parts of the country at this time, when we allow for the differing sizes and location of the churches and oratories, the varying capacity and training of the clergy, and the differences in the people themselves. Yet, remembering that the clergy were all monastic and therefore belonged to disciplined brotherhoods, we must also not be surprised to find a basic similarity in the worship everywhere, in churches great and small throughout the land. It is easy in retrospect to exaggerate the differences and to miss the underlying unity in the worship of this period. The Stowe Missal therefore conveys to us worship we may take as typical in Scotland and Ireland in the eighth to tenth centuries in a great church.

Before the service began, while the ministers vested and prepared the elements of bread and wine and water for the sacred rite (by this time the offerings in kind had disappeared, and the elements were prepared before the service), fairly elaborate prayers of confession and approach were said and a very brief litany was sung. The rite proper began with the introit or 'ingressa', a psalm sung antiphonally by the choir concluding with the doxology, while the clergy entered and proceeded to the holy table.

After the introit, the celebrant saluted the people saying, *Dominus vobiscum*, with the response *Et cum spiritu tuo*.

[1] *The Books of the Latin Liturgy*, p. 107.

Then he called them to prayer, and said a series of collects, for in Celtic use the number of collects had much
increased. Hymns were then sung, the Celtic love of
music causing several to be sung successively at this point,
and we find mentioned the *Tersanctus, Benedictus Dominus,
Kyries*, and the *Gloria in excelsis* or 'Imnus Angelicus' as
it was called.[1] Again several collects were said, including
collects of the day.

Now came the lessons from Holy Scripture: first, a
lesson from the Old Testament, which might be followed
by such a hymn as *Benedicite*.[2] Next the epistle was read,
followed by another series of collects interspersed by
psalms and alleluias, after which a bidding prayer with
collects was said in the manner described earlier. Thereafter, the chalice was unveiled—in many Gallican rites
the preparation of the elements and the admixture of
water took place here, in an elaborate setting of prayer
—and Psalm 141.2, 'Let my prayer be set forth before
thee as incense'[3] was sung thrice during this action, followed by a second chant, 'Tui, domine, sanctificator,
omnipotens, et benedic hoc sacrificium preparatum tibi'
also sung thrice. Then the gospel, after a procession with
lights, is sung by the deacon, followed by prayers and
chants. Some two-thirds of a page is missing here in the
Stowe Missal, but judging from contemporary Gallican
practice, such chants as *Benedictus es* or *Tersanctus* were
sung here; and after that the sermon would be preached,
followed by another series of collects and St. John 6.53-56,
'Jesus said . . . Except ye eat the flesh of the Son of Man',

---

[1] The hymns, 'Holy and Mighty, Holy and Immortal', 'Blessed be the
Lord God of Israel', 'Lord have mercy', and 'Glory be to God on high',
all of which occur in Gallican liturgies.

[2] The Song of the Three Children.

[3] Warren is of opinion that incense was not used in the Celtic services
(op. cit., pp. 127-8) though its use is scriptural and was common elsewhere;
more evidence than he adduces would be required to prove its absence.

&c., sung no doubt as an anthem and invitatory. Then the Nicene Creed was sung.[1]

The second part of the service, the liturgy of the faithful, begins with the offertory during which the elements are fully unveiled, while Psalm 85.7, 'Shew us thy mercy, O Lord, and grant us thy salvation' is sung thrice, and the paten and cup are offered with prayers and elevated. Then the diptychs (a list of names of the departed) are read by the deacon, the celebrant saying a prayer *post nomina* commemorating with thanks apostles, martyrs, and confessors, 'remembering especially him whose relics lie below the altar,[2] and those whose festal day it is, together with 'all our departed bishops, priests, deacons, beloved ones, children, and all who died in penitence'.

Now the prayer of consecration begins introduced by salutation and *Sursum corda*, and a majestic preface is sung in praise of God, and, concelebrating with angels and all the heavenly host and blessed seraphim, the celebrant leads into the *Sanctus* and *Benedictus qui venit* with hosannas. The prayer is taken up again by the celebrant in a *post sanctus*, and he continues aloud with the Roman canon[3] which had been adopted in the Stowe Missal by the ninth or tenth century with a few Celtic peculiarities and long catalogues of Celtic saints and others.

At the conclusion of the canon, the fraction is performed elaborately in the Gallican manner by two priests

---

[1] Not introduced in Roman use till eleventh century, though in some Gallican rites (e.g. in France and Spain) it was introduced in 589 by the Third Council of Toledo; it is unlikely to have been used by the Celtic peoples earlier than the ninth century.

[2] In early times churches were often built at the site of a saint's burial place or martyrdom, the holy table standing above his tomb; and later relics were placed beneath the holy table or the mensa, a custom which became universal in the West.

[3] It is entitled *Canon dominicus papae Gilasi*: its inclusion in this missal is not evidence that it was universally or even widely used in Celtic worship at this time. The point cannot be precisely determined.

('confractio') who may have concelebrated, the consecrated bread being symbolically divided into from five
to thirteen pieces, and placed in the form of a cross, and
at festivals into as many as sixty-five pieces. Meantime
anthems were sung with alleluias and collects said, and
the celebrant said the Lord's Prayer with an introductory
sentence (called the protocol), and an addition (called
the embolism). Then, following Roman custom the pax
was given, but the formula used is drawn from the
Mozarabic rite; thereafter the celebrant blessed the
people.

While *Agnus Dei* was sung, the celebrant received communion. During the communion of the people in both
kinds was sung a long series of antiphons (verses from the
psalms with alleluias), Psalm 26, 'Judge me, O Lord',
being imbedded in their midst, the whole ending in a
triumphant invocation with alleluias. A brief post-
communion thanksgiving *Gratias tibi agimus* which occurs
in several Gallican MSS. follows, and in some earlier rites
a deacon's litany was added; after which the deacon dismissed the people, using a familiar Gallican formula,
Missa acta est. In pace.

Though this description does not include every small
detail and ceremony, it will be recognized how greatly
the rite has been lengthened and elaborated. It must
have been a truly moving service providing sustained
opportunity for devotion, and the constant recurrence of
alleluias at solemn moments kept the faithful in mind of
the victory of the risen living Christ. The rite at every
point, however, shows evidence of that eclecticism of
which we have spoken, and the tendency of the Celtic
monks when abroad to gather such rites and ceremonies
as appealed to them, and to add them to their rite.

In all this, reference has been made only to the chief
Sunday worship, but behind and surrounding it lay the

whole discipline of daily prayer, with offices, litanies, and hymns, together with the discipline of confession, penance, and fasting, all of which were rigorously strict and excessively severe in the Celtic Church, as the old penitentials show.[1] Together with this was the Celtic love of the Holy Scriptures, and the elaborate sanctification of things and places.[2] We must be aware of all this if we are to understand Celtic worship and piety, to see how it entered into and sanctified every area of life.

Of the music to which the rites were set, no trace now remains. It has been thought by some to have more closely resembled the music of the East rather than the West, but this is a very doubtful conjecture, more emotional than factual. It was almost certainly closely related to what was common throughout the Gallican rites, with Celtic embellishments, and typical Celtic tunes set to the hymns, in the use and variety of which the Celts excelled.

The churches in northern Britain were generally built with the sanctuary towards the east, but this was not invariably so, and even the course of a river could affect the siting of a church. It appears that the celebrant commonly celebrated standing in front of the altar and facing eastwards. Warren believes this to have been universal in Celtic churches, and in support of his view refers to a description of light falling from behind on the heads of the clergy as they stood before the altar:

Sed illi post Evangelii recitationem viderunt quendam igneum globum et valde luminosum de vertice sancti Columbae ante altare stantis et sacram oblationem consecrantis tamdiu

---

[1] J. T. M'Neill, *Medieval Handbooks of Penance*, N.Y., 1938. It is interesting to note that the system of the private confessional as opposed to public confession and discipline derives from Celtic usage, and was borrowed by Rome from the Celts (Ivo M. Clark, *A History of Church Discipline in Scotland*, pp. 28 sqq.).

[2] See Grub, *Ecclesiastical History of Scotland*, I, pp. 150 sqq.

ardere, et ad instar alicujus columnae sursum ascendere donec eadem perficerentur sacro-sancta mysteria.[1]

But it would be dangerous to dogmatize from such evidence, in itself not wholly free from ambiguity[2] and perhaps more romantic than strictly accurate. I am disposed to believe it possible, and even probable, that the basilican method of celebration may have continued for a considerable period in the Celtic Church, it and the eastwards position—increasingly the more general of the two—existing side by side.

Speaking of orientation in general, Davies usefully summarizes the matter when he says that there is no need to account for it

by asserting with Strzygowski the influence of Armenia and its Mazdean sun temples. Clement of Alexandria provides sufficient ground for its adoption when he says: 'the east is an image of the day of birth, and from that point the light which has shone forth at first from the darkness increases, and there has also dawned on those involved in darkness a day of the knowledge of truth'. In close harmony with this is the reference to Christ as the 'Dayspring from on high' and the 'Light of the world' to which Chrysostom calls the attention of his hearers. Other reasons for or, more correctly, deductions from the practice are that in praying to the east the soul is hoping for restoration to its ancient home in Paradise through Christ the Second Adam, and that Christians are looking for their Lord's return, since the coming of the Son of Man will be like the 'lightning that cometh out of the east and shineth even unto the west'.[3]

It is not possible to say how many ministers, apart

[1] Cuminius, *Vita S. Columbae*, cap. xii.

[2] What, e.g., does 'ante altare' mean precisely? It need not mean between the altar and the people. The light might have been from the rising sun, falling through an east window, and it would then have fallen on his back if he was using the basilican posture and have created the illusion of a ball of fire rising from his head.

[3] op. cit., pp. 82-83.

from the celebrant(s), assisted, or precisely how they did so; but it is clear that for many centuries there was no fixed practice of three ministers—celebrant, deacon, and sub-deacon. It would seem that something like the old Roman method, described on an earlier page,[1] was followed; the function of a deacon, as in the early liturgies, appears to have been to guide or represent the people in their devotions rather than specifically to assist the celebrant; and there were no doubt other ministers and servers as circumstances allowed or required. In the litany of the Stowe Missal minor orders are mentioned only collectively if at all, and the Pope is not specifically mentioned: 'Pro pastore, N., episcopo, et omnibus episcopis, et praespeteris [presbyteris], et diace, et omni clero.' In the consecration prayer itself, which is the Roman canon in the Stowe Missal, the Pope is mentioned, but he is not mentioned in the older prayer quoted; the canon was introduced into Scotland and Ireland about the ninth century, even though it was not universally used until a later date.

The vestments of the clergy,[2] as can be seen chiefly from illuminated MSS. and old stones, were closely similar to those in later use, but not so formalized in strict shape; and we may be confident from our knowledge of Celtic art that they were beautifully made and ornamented.

We may conclude by glancing briefly at the church-buildings in use in Scotland, say till the eleventh century, and these will help to give us some idea of the surroundings and setting of the rite, and clarify our picture.

St. Ninian's church at Whithorn was built of stone and lime in the manner of northern Gaul, and in Scotland was considered a great novelty and wonder. This was

[1] p. 4 supra.
[2] Warren, op. cit., pp. 112 sqq. On vestments in general, see H. Norris, *Church Vestments, their Origin and Development*, various publications of the Alcuin Club, and Dearmer, *The Ornaments of the Ministers*.

because most churches in Scotland and Ireland were for centuries, as in Scandinavia, built of wood. In parts of the country where timber was not available they were sometimes built of earth, and wooden churches were often (perhaps normally) wattled. The first buildings at Iona, St. Adamnan implies, were wooden and wattled; and similar churches were built by Celtic missionaries on the continent. Stone churches began to occur frequently after the sixth century, built in the manner of dry-stane dykes, and probably stopped with earth; others were built of rough stone, bedded in clay.

All these churches we should nowadays judge to be very small, and many of them, notable in their day, were tiny ill-lighted oratories, as we see by ruins and remnants. Even the great church of St. Patrick at Teltown in Meath was but 60 ft. in length, some 30 ft. shorter than the ships in which the Vikings crossed the seas (how vast and menacing these ships must have seemed!); and the first cathedral at Armagh (*c.* 445) was only 100 ft. in length. In Scotland there is no evidence that there were larger churches: all ancient remains are small.

What were they like? Apart from the ruins of many churches discovered or exposed by archeologists,[1] we have one description of a wooden church at Kildare,[2] as it appeared in the eighth century.

In this church repose the bodies of both Bishop Coulaeth and the Virgin St. Bridget [we are told] on the right and left of the decorated altar, deposited in ornaments adorned with various embellishments of gold and silver and gems and precious stones, with crowns of gold and silver depending from above. As the number of the faithful of both sexes had increased, the church occupied a spacious area and was elevated to a menacing height and adorned with painted

---

[1] See, e.g., Ian C. Hannah, *Story of Scotland in Stone.*
[2] Warren, op. cit., pp. 89 sqq.

pictures, having within it three oratories, large and separated by partitions of planks under the one roof of the greater house, wherein one partition, decorated and painted with figures and covered with linen hangings, extended along the breadth in the eastern part of the church from one to other of the outside walls.[1] This partition has at its extremity two doors: and through the door at the right the senior bishop, with his regular clergy and those deputed to the sacred ministry of offering holy and dominical sacrifices, enters the sanctuary; through the other door at the left none enter but the abbess with her virgins and faithful widows when going to participate in the Body and Blood of Jesus Christ. Another partition, dividing the pavement of the house into two equal parts, extends from the eastern[2] end to the transverse screen lying across its breadth. The church has in it many windows,[3] and one ornamented doorway on the right side through which the priests and faithful men enter the church, and another on the left side through which the congregation of virgins and faithful women are accustomed to enter. And thus in one very great temple a multitude of people of different orders and ranks, sex and situation, separated by screens, in different order but with one mind worship Almighty God.

[1] This partition divided the sanctuary from the nave, concealing the holy table from the sight of the people. The description of the altar with 'crown depending from above' suggests that it had over it a canopy or ciborium, customary enough elsewhere at that time.

[2] As Warren suggests (op. cit., p. 90), 'eastern' is clearly an error for 'western'. Mention of this partition or screen reminds us that it was universal for centuries at Christian worship (as also in the synagogues) to separate the men and women (cf. many liturgical documents, and Davies, op. cit.), a practice that survived the Reformation and persisted in Scotland in some places till within living memory. It was common also on the continent after the Reformation, as old prints show. The north door of a church was for long regarded as the women's door, and where there were altars flanking the chancel arch they had dedications appropriate to male and female saints. See also p. 97, n. 3 infra.

[3] The windows were probably not glazed. 'Bede assigns the first introduction of glass and painting into England, A.D. 676, to Benedict Biscop, and he had to bring glaziers from Gaul' (Warren, op. cit., p. 90). It is most unlikely to have reached Ireland or Scotland at this time, and its use did not become universal for many centuries.

C

The decorations of the church were rich, and finely wrought; enough of Celtic ornament has survived to indicate the skill and beauty of the craftsmanship, examples of which may be seen in national and other collections.

Altars were of wood or stone, and seem sometimes to have stood side by side,[1] and were much smaller in width and length than the later altars of medieval churches, and were characterized by a boldly projecting mensa or top slab, as we know from the few that have survived.[2]

In the earlier period, altars were often but not always concealed from the worshippers by a partition, screen, or wall, with doors or curtains. This has already appeared in the description of the church at Kildare. Another example is to be found, I believe, in the ancient Celtic chapel of the 'bee-hive' type described by W. Fraser Darling in his *Naturalist on Rona*,[3] the ruins of which he was able to restore in the dry-stane fashion in which they were built.

The chapel consisted of two parts: what he calls the hermit's cell, but which I suggest was the sanctuary where the holy table anciently stood; and what he calls the church, which I believe to have been originally the nave. These were divided by a wall with a central door; and this is exactly what we should expect to find in a church of that type in which an arch could not have been built or a wide opening constructed by the builders, even had they wished to do either of these things. Probably they did not so wish, but followed a pattern common not

[1] Such phrases as 'inter altaria' and 'inter ipsa sacrosancta altaria' suggest this. Altars in medieval churches were multiplied, but for a different reason (see p. 39 infra).

[2] An excellent example of the tenth or eleventh century is the nave altar preserved in the monastic church at Varnhem, Sweden; and an early medieval representation of a similar altar is set in the porch gable at St. Mary's parish church, Whitekirk, East Lothian.

[3] pp. 38 sqq.

merely to Scotland but to other parts of Christendom in this and earlier times. The ground plan of the Chapel of Announa in North Africa,[1] for example, suggests that such a device was not unknown where skilled builders were not always accessible, and in some places it may have been preferred where they were available. In the Celtic chapel described by Fraser Darling, altar stones remain on the nave side of the dividing wall in front of the door, but seem to be of a later date than the building itself. This again suggests to me what we should expect at a later time as consonant with changes which took place elsewhere, namely that an altar was placed in the nave in front of the door within easy view of the people; examples of such nave altars exist in many parts of Europe, from at least the twelfth century onwards. A partition immediately before the altar was early common to Eastern and Western Christendom for a considerable period. This dividing barrier gradually disappeared in Western Christendom for the most part, or at least was so designed that the action could be seen through it; but in Eastern Christendom a solid screen upon which icons could be displayed came to be preferred.[2]

Outside the church and contained within a wall was from time immemorial the burying-place of the community, but burials also often took place within the church, the floors of which for centuries in Scotland were normally earthen.

Each church also had its bell. In early times the bells were portable, and continued in use in some parts of Scotland until well into the nineteenth century for certain purposes long after bells had been fixed in the towers.

[1] Davies, op. cit., p. 134; and see A. C. Champneys, *Irish Eccl. Architecture* (1910) for descriptions and plans of early Celtic churches.

[2] This is an over-simplified but broadly accurate account. Details are discussed in Davies, op. cit., pp. 90-92, 122, 126-8, 134; on later developments in England, see A. Vallance, *Greater English Church Screens*.

Such a bell, for example, still exists in my own parish, having come from the old Norman church at Tyninghame, and others are to be found in museums. St. Ninian was said to have been famous for his bell, and it seems to have been common custom for the early missionaries to these islands to carry their bells with them to summon the people to instruction and prayer. Later, hand bells were sacring bells or lych bells. The lych bells were the medieval predecessors of the post-Reformation mort bells.

Such is a general picture of worship in the early Scottish Church. We pass now to the days of Queen Margaret, then move on to the eve of the Reformation.

II

Medieval Worship in Scotland

WHEN about 1070 Malcolm III married as his second wife Margaret, a princess of England and sister of Edgar the Atheling, a new stage began in the history of the Scottish Church. Margaret had been born in Hungary, coming later to England, and both these countries were more closely under the influence and authority of Rome than was Scotland, and in their worship therefore nearer to the contemporary use of the Roman Church than were the Scottish rites.

But Scotland too gradually became more closely linked with Rome in her fight to be independent of the English crown and the English Church. The Archbishop of York from time to time renewed his claim of authority over the Scottish Church; and, largely because of this, the Scots had adopted St. Andrew as their patron, for they could then appeal with moving effect to the Pope who sat in the chair of Peter, Andrew's brother whom Andrew had brought to Jesus.[1] Thus, although the Scots allowed obedience in many things to the rising claims of the papacy, their real policy through the coming centuries was to preserve the independence of their Church and nation and to be dominated by neither the Pope nor the English king. Within this was also a second struggle, as the years passed, between the Scottish Church and the Scottish crown; and both Church and crown often found

[1] See Hannay, *St. Andrew.*

it convenient to be able to appeal to the Pope. Accordingly, the ties between the Scottish Church and the papacy grew gradually firmer, and the influence of the Roman rite of the period made itself increasingly felt. This connexion and influence Margaret sedulously fostered, and it was she who laid its real foundations.

Queen Margaret was a woman of deep and sincere piety, who loved utterly her Lord and His Church. The details of her life are well known, for her biographer was her confessor; and we need say no more here than that she was genuinely and zealously concerned to cleanse, maintain, and strengthen the Scottish Church. This included its worship, which was indeed much in need of reform. One reform she desired was to increase among the people the practice of communicating regularly and frequently. We are to remember that although the eucharist was celebrated weekly, and in many places daily, throughout Western Christendom at this time, the people themselves had for centuries past fallen into the habit of receiving communion very infrequently (council after council had marked this, and sought to reform it), once a year being the normal pious practice.[1] Even the yearly Easter communion Margaret found now neglected in Scotland.[2]

Margaret learned also that there was much diversity in the manner of celebrating mass, as indeed we should expect in the Scottish Church of the time; but she discovered, further, that some were even accustomed to celebrate mass with 'nescio quo ritu barbaro, contrary to the custom of the whole Church'. Now what was this 'ritus

[1] See pp. 51 sqq. infra.
[2] In contrast to earlier practice, e.g. Adamnan, *Vita S. Columbae*, ii. 39: 'Ut in Paschali solemnitate ad altare accedas, et eucharistiam sumas . . . Et post peractam Paschae sollemnitatem in qua jussus ad altare accessit.' In op. cit., iii. 23, Easter is described as 'Laetitiae festivitas'. See Warren, op. cit., p. 7.

barbarus'? 'Ritus' refers to the words not to the actions
of the service, and 'barbarus' in eleventh century Latin,
when related to words, can mean only 'vernacular'; it would
appear then that a 'ritus barbarus' is a vernacular rite,
and that it cannot mean, as some have thought, remembering their classical Latin, a rite barbarously celebrated.
There is, it is true, no trace of any text of the mass in
the vernacular to support this translation, but that need
not surprise us, for such services were, we may be sure,
conducted only in remote places and not in the great
centres. It is indeed possible that they were never committed to writing at all, but were translated or loosely
and roughly paraphrased in part or whole by the celebrant as he said the service so that his remote and simple
folk might understand. To celebrate in the vernacular
was, as Turgot indignantly points out, 'contrary to the
custom of the whole Church', so that 'henceforth there
appeared no one in the whole race of Scots who dared
to do such a thing'.

Margaret desired also to bring some uniformity of
practice into the Scottish Church, and though the description of what she did is by no means clear, it is likely
that she sought to introduce as a standard a rite based
upon that used in the province of York, for she is said
to have made the Scottish episcopate subject to the Archbishop of York.[1]

Some have thought that she introduced the Sarum rite
into Scotland, but this is highly improbable, for it was
not issued until 1085, eight years before her death; indeed,
the see of Salisbury was founded only in 1075,[2] and it
was not till three years later that the great St. Osmund
began his reforming and organizing work there. We know

[1] York claimed that she had done so, but proof is lacking. However,
whether or no, it was inevitable that the northern province, especially
via Durham, should be influential.

[2] Procter and Frere, *A New History of the Book of Common Prayer*, p. 15.

also that the Sarum use was not introduced in Glasgow till some fifty years after Margaret's death. It is clear, therefore, that it was only gradually adopted in Scotland; and further we are to remember that the Sarum rite itself was not definitively fixed until the early thirteenth century under Richard Poole, first as dean and later as bishop, who issued a full code of liturgical rules. The Roman canon, of course, had begun to appear in Scottish liturgies long before this, and was coming to be preferred everywhere throughout the West.

Thus after Margaret's time, while it is impossible to trace the exact steps, a growing conformity to the Sarum use appears in Scottish worship, and, even if it was not used in every particular, its influence was sufficiently strong from the mid-twelfth century gradually to suppress the diverse Scottish uses, and to accomplish a general, if not absolutely particular, uniformity throughout the Scottish Church. This was furthered by Margaret's sons who in succession ruled for fifty-six years after her death, lived in devotion to her ideals, and carried steadily forward the ecclesiastical revolution initiated by her.[1]

Nevertheless, it must be made clear that the process of the growing ascendancy of the use of Sarum extended over some three or four centuries, and there was by no means complete uniformity. Liturgical uniformity in the strict sense is a Reformed and Tridentine conception unknown before the sixteenth century. Witness to this is abundant in liturgical texts throughout the history of the Church; and it is worth noting that express mention is made of this fact in the Book of Common Prayer in the section 'Concerning the Service of the Church' where it is said: 'Whereas there hath been great diversity in saying and singing in churches within this realm, . . . now from henceforth, all the whole realm shall have but one

[1] Duke, *History of Church of Scotland*, p. 78.

use.' What was true of England was true also of Scotland, and of the whole Western Church—and for that matter of the Eastern Church also.

It is not necessary here to trace the vicissitudes of the Scottish Church through the successive centuries of its long struggle for reasonable autonomy against Roman or English domination. The general policy was to maintain in the Pope a friendly ally and to yield to him a general and respectful obedience without allowing him to gain excessive power; and by his help to remain independent alike of Scottish royal and English political and ecclesiastical domination. We are concerned only with worship, and as we have seen Scottish use conformed more and more to Sarum, the dominant and most orderly rite of the period; and it is not till the early years of the sixteenth century that we find the great Bishop Elphinstone of Aberdeen shaping out a Scottish rite, itself a reform of Sarum. But it did not reach completion, and his reforms were related to the daily offices of the Church and not to the eucharist.[1]

From such fragments, however, as this: 'The Culdees (Keledri) in a corner of their church which was very small used to celebrate their own office after their own fashion',[2] referring to a period fifty years after Margaret, it was thought by some, for example, Grub, Cunningham, Hume Brown, and Warren,[3] that Celtic worship persisted after Margaret's time, and in one or two places, St. Andrews for example, till the fourteenth century,

---

[1] A copy of Elphinstone's Breviary is in the University Library, Aberdeen. In this attempt to reach uniformity in Scottish worship, Chepman and Millar were granted privilege to print service-books 'eftir our awin Scottis use', i.e. those composed or projected by Elphinstone. As an indication of the ascendancy Salisbury had gained by this time in Scotland, it is interesting (if disappointing) to note that this refers to the suppression of only the 'bukis of Salusbery use' (*Source Book of Scottish History*, ii, pp. 117-18).

[2] *Chron. Picts and Scots*, edited by Skene, p. 190.   [3] op. cit., p. 8.

preserving 'a state of purity and simplicity, before it had
been corrupted by Rome'.

But this is not so. In the first place 'office' refers almost
certainly to the hours' services, and not to the eucharist.
And secondly the Culdees were originally 'companions or
followers of God', a strict group within the Celtic (Irish
and Scots) monastic system who lived as hermits. It was
not a general name for Celtic monastics, but a particular
name for a specific group within them. They were mostly
absorbed in the twelfth century (under David) 'into the
Augustinian Order, and transformed into Canons'. At
first severely strict, they degenerated, and in the twelfth
century we find a little group at St. Andrews, thirteen in
number, 'who lived after their own fancy and the traditions of men, rather than after the precepts of the holy
Fathers'.[1] They were married, held property, and transmitted their ecclesiastical endowments to their children.[2]
The Culdees have no significance whatever, liturgically
speaking, and certainly were not the custodians and pre-
servers of an ancient Scottish rite.

To provide a general picture of worship in a great
church in Scotland in medieval times, we may describe
the normative service of high mass according to the
Sarum rite.[3]

The ministers privately prepare for the service while
vesting, saying the *Veni Creator* with versicle and response,
the collect for purity ('Almighty God, unto whom all
hearts'), Ps. 43 with antiphon, verse 4*a*, three-fold *Kyries*,
the Lord's Prayer, and an *Ave Maria*.

The service begins when the choir[4] sings the introit or

[1] Haddan and Stubbs, *Councils*, ii., pp. 179-80, quoting *Hist. Eccles. S. Andr.*

[2] See Duke, op. cit., pp. 67-70; and more recently and thoroughly
G. W. S. Barrow's exploding of this myth in *Jour. of Eccles. Hist.*, iii.

[3] Text, e.g., in Procter and Frere, op. cit., pp. 282 sqq.

[4] Consisting of members of an order or of secular clergy, with some
singing boys standing in front of the stalls or grouped about the quire lectern.

'officium', now a part of a psalm with antiphon and *Gloria Patri*. While this proceeds, the ministers, at the altar steps, speaking in an undertone make confession one to another and receive and give absolution, say brief versicles and responses, give to each other the kiss of peace, and approaching the altar say a collect. Then, signing the altar with the sign of the cross, the celebrant says, 'In the name' . . . The singers now go on to the *Kyries* sung nine-fold, and the *Gloria in excelsis*. Meanwhile, the deacon fills the thurible with incense, and bids the celebrant bless it, after which he kisses it and passes it to the celebrant who censes the altar in the centre and at both ends. Thereafter, the deacon censes the celebrant; and they kiss the linen cloth upon the altar. Then, facing the altar with their backs to the people, they go to the right end of it, and say the introit and *Kyries*, which the choir is singing; after which they go to the sedilia (seats usually built in the wall at the south side of the sanctuary), and remain there till the choir is ready to sing the *Gloria*, which the ministers begin from the centre of the altar and continue to sing in a low voice from the right end of the altar.

When the *Gloria* ends, the celebrant signs his face with the sign of the cross, turns to the people, and, raising his forearms a little, joins his hands and says *Dominus vobiscum*, to which the choir replies *Et cum spiritu tuo*. Then turning towards the altar he says *Oremus* and the collect of the day; memorials may follow, but not more than seven collects are to be said at this point, each preceded by an *Oremus* and completed by a doxology, *per dominum*, &c. Meanwhile, after the introit, an acolyte has set aside the bread and wine and water to be used at the eucharist, and another brings a basin of water and a hand-towel.

As the last collect begins, the sub-deacon goes down through the midst of the quire to read the epistle from a raised place. Afterwards, two boys in surplices, after inclining towards the altar, go to the raised place, and facing each other begin the antiphonal singing of the gradual; and when the gradual ends two others of senior status lead the alleluias, by this time an elaborate piece of music. And thereafter, the sequence or tract was sung in the form of a hymn. Then the deacon censes the central part of the altar, and receiving from the celebrant the gospel-book which reposes on the mensa, stands humbly before him and asks his blessing, and the celebrant says: 'The Lord be in your heart and in your lips as you proclaim the holy gospel, in the name of the Father and of the Son and of the Holy Ghost, Amen.' And the deacon, preceded by a thurifer and candle-bearer (acolytes or servers with incense and candle) goes to the raised place, facing north.[1] Then, after saluting the people (*Dominus vobiscum*, &c.), he makes the sign of the cross with his thumb over the book, his forehead, and his breast, and sings the gospel of the day; after which he kisses the book, and returns with it to the altar.

Thereafter, the celebrant from the centre of the altar begins the Nicene Creed, and the choir sings it, 'not alternately, but as a full choir', and the salutation and *Oremus* follow, but the prayer by this time has disappeared.[2]

Now the liturgy of the faithful begins, and the choir sings the offertory, part of a psalm with antiphon sung from side to side. The celebrant meanwhile says it in a low voice, and the deacon presents to him the paten and chalice with the elements of bread and wine, kissing his hands lightly; the celebrant places the chalice in the centre of the altar, then bowing for a moment lifts it in both hands as a sacrifice offered to God, and says the

[1] See p. 5 supra.   [2] See p. 5 supra.

offertory collect, *Suscipe Sancta Trinitas*. Replacing it on
the altar, he covers it over with white linen cloths, called
the corporals, and puts the bread decently on the corporals in front of the chalice which contains wine to
which water has been added. Then, kissing the paten,
he places it on the altar to the right of the chalice, and
almost covers it with the corporals. When he has done
this, he takes the thurible from the deacon, censes the
holy elements and says the brief prayer *Dirigatur* ('May
my prayer go up before thee as incense') and censes
himself. After which, he goes to the right end of the
altar, and washes his hands, saying, *Munda me Domine*;
and coming to the centre of the altar, he bows down his
head and body, joins his hands and says *In spiritu humili-
tatis*; then, rising up he kisses the altar at the right of
the holy elements, blesses them, and signs himself saying
In nomine.

He now turns to the people and says silently *Orate
fratres*, and the ministers reply privately *Spiritus Sancti
gratia*. Then, turning to the altar, the celebrant says
the secrets (prayers said silently) appropriate in number
and order to the collects said before the epistle, beginning with the *Haec sacra*; and when he reaches the end
of the prayers, he raises his voice and says the conclusion
aloud. Thereafter, the subdeacon receives the offerings
and paten from the hands of the deacon.

Turning to the people, the celebrant salutes them,
Dominus vobiscum, to which they respond, *Et cum spiritu
tuo*, and lifting up his hands sings the *Sursum corda*, the
choir responding; then goes on to sing the preface, *Vere
dignum*, and so to the *Sanctus*, which the choir takes up,
and the *Benedictus qui venit*, while the celebrant goes on
silently with the remainder of the consecration prayer
(the Roman canon), during which he does the manual
acts and makes the elevation at the *Qui pridie* (the words

of institution), and the prayer ends with an ecphonesis, when the celebrant raises his voice at the concluding words, *per omnia saecula saeculorum*. Then he says *Oremus* and the Lord's Prayer silently, raising his voice at 'lead us not into temptation', the choir responding 'But deliver us from evil', the celebrant saying 'Amen' silently and continuing silently with the embolism *Libera nos*.

Then with ceremonies and prayers two fractions take place, and the commixture of the bread to the wine, the prayers ending with an ecphonesis; and if a bishop is present, he then blesses the people. Thereafter, the kiss of peace is given to the ministers, and taken by the sub-deacon to the choir.

Agnus Dei is now sung, the deacon and subdeacon standing each on a step below the celebrant, and one below the other, and on the celebrant's right. The celebrant signs a piece of the consecrated Bread with the cross, and adds it to the chalice saying *Haec sacrosancta commixtio* and before the pax, *Domine sancte*. Then after the prayers *Deus pater, fons et origo, Domine Jesu Christe*, and *Corporis et sanguinis*, he bows down and says to the Bread ('ad corpus dicat') *Ave in aeternum*, and receives the Bread, and similarly saluting the Wine, he receives it; then gives thanks *Gratias tibi ago*. Meantime the communion anthem is sung by the choir, following upon the *Agnus Dei*; and the ministers likewise receive communion; after which the celebrant goes on with the ablution of the holy vessels while prayers are said secretly.

Then he says the post-communion prayers, in number and order appropriate to the prayers said before the epistle: and the people are dismissed with *Ite, missa est*, and the celebrant bowing down before the altar says the last prayer *Placeat tibi*, and rising up signs himself with the cross and says *In nomine*. The ministers and servers now leave the church in the order in which they entered, the celebrant reading the last Gospel *In principio* (St. John 1.1-14) before he goes.

This is a brief description of a solemn mass, of which every minute part is detailed for the celebrant and his ministers. It will be noticed by those who study it carefully that the Holy Scriptures are woven into its very fabric in psalmody, readings, and prayers, and the propers for the day are especially rich in Scriptural reference and interpretation. Indeed, the loss of the propers, not yet fully recovered, was without doubt the greatest Scriptural loss at the Reformation. The music, too, if it had by this time become somewhat over-elaborate, was still a superb vehicle of devotion; the ceremonial was supremely solemn and the whole action sublime in dignity and reverence, rich in colour and symbol, and profoundly devotional. Disciplined and carefully delivered from exotic excess, in the setting of a great medieval Gothic church the service moved grandly and with deep dramatic effect to its tremendous climax of oblation.

Despite all this, however, the worship had become remote from the people. It was said throughout in Latin, a language which now for centuries had been known only by the educated few. If a sermon was preached, and this was no longer a regular part of the service, it would be in the vernacular together with certain prayers said before and after it; and the Scriptures might be read again in the common tongue of the people before the sermon in a little vernacular service called the prone embedded in the mass,[1] but this was not a fixed feature, nor was it everywhere used. The ceremonial, august, symbolical, and meaningful to the initiated, was not understood by the great body of the people, who could not therefore

---

[1] The 'prone' is described by Brightman, *English Rite*, ii, pp. 1020 sqq. His notion that the continental Reformed services derived from the prone cannot be sustained; for texts see my *John Knox's Genevan Service-Book*, p. 17.

intelligently follow the service.[1] The elevation was for them the climactic point, when bells were rung, and they prostrated themselves, but the remainder of the service to most of the laity was sheer mystery. Thus popular attendance fell off, as the people could not share in the great action, fundamentally transformed into a dramatic spectacle and no longer an action of common worship.

Further, such a service could be performed only in the great churches—cathedrals, abbeys, and collegiate churches, amply staffed with clergy and choirs. In small parish churches, the facilities were lacking. A sung mass with celebrant and servers only was therefore devised, but even this could not be used in a great number of parishes because of the musical incapacity of the clergy and the lack of trained singers.

There was also a growing irreverence and slovenliness too often evident in places high and low; churches were neglected, frontals and hangings dilapidated, and movement and conversation took place during the action; and often it was burlesqued in a variety of ways such as by the Abbot of Misrule. All this need not be detailed here, but will be found *inter alia* easily accessible in the volumes of Hay Fleming and C. G. Coulton,[2] together, alas, with many other abuses that grew up within the Church, paralysing and soiling it.

Because of the difficulty of singing high mass in the

[1] Nowadays, when all are literate, the people by being instructed in the meaning of the ceremonial, may follow mass, high or low, in their missals which have Latin in one column and the vernacular in the other; and can thus take an active and attentive part in the prayers. But before the Reformation, missals were not available as printing was but newly-discovered (indeed missals did not exist as we know them in their modern form), and translations of the service were rare; and if they had been generally available, the great majority of the people, being illiterate, could have made no use of them. The modern missal, with its parallel columns of Latin and the vernacular, is in fact a reply to the vernacular service-books instituted by the Reformers of the sixteenth century.

[2] Hay Fleming, *The Reformation in Scotland*; C. G. Coulton's medieval studies.

smaller churches, and as the service itself became remote
from the people's understanding—and related also to the
doctrine of each mass as an act of merit having a quanti-
tative value in itself—there sprang up in the ninth or
tenth centuries a habit of saying mass with one priest
and a server, and this came to be known as low mass.
It required no staff of clergy and no trained singers; and
because it was in an unknown tongue it could be said
silently and therefore with great rapidity; the ceremonial
could be reduced to a minimum and quickly performed.
And where many masses had to be said[1] when foundations were provided for the dead, this method of recitation
was swift, convenient, and held theologically to be of
equal efficacy. Because of its brevity and convenience it
became the popular service, and people attended at
it rather than at high mass. Thus the whole service
degenerated into an incomprehensible action, inaudible,
mysterious, performed by one on behalf of the many.
The nadir of pre-Reformation worship had come.

Altars were multiplied in the churches, but the high
altar was neglected, and as Gavin has said,

In east and west alike frequent communion had become
exceptional. The idea of the eucharist as the impetratory
Sacrifice of our Lord's Body and Blood for the living and the
dead has become overwhelmingly predominant. By the early
middle ages there has arisen in the west 'low' mass—one said
by a priest with a server or other person acting for the people
as congregation to answer the responses. Church architecture changes: chantry chapels are built, where private masses
on 'foundations' can be offered with special remembrance of
the people for whom they are 'offered'. The ancient usages
of the liturgy as the service of all the people, in which all
had both an active and essential part, have been gradually

[1] Cf. my *Outline of Christian Worship*, pp. 67-8, and references to authorities, which detail the grave abuses related to low mass; see also A. Fortescue,
The Mass.

D

altered—whether by abrogation, transformation, or steriliza-
tion—in keeping with a policy of regimented uniformity under
the pressure of the Roman see. The language is symbolic of
the worship. The dead tongue suggests the mystery which
invests the rite, so much of which is transacted secretly or in
a whisper. At the fourth Lateran Council of 1215, transubstantiation was defined as a dogma, yearly confession and
Easter Communion were made of universal obligation, and
the beginning of the cultus of the Blessed Sacrament con-
nected with elevation and exposition appear about that date.[1]

Sermons were seldom preached by the parish clergy;
oftener perhaps in the great churches, but rarely—once
or twice a year—in the parish churches where preaching
was beyond the capacity of most of the secular clergy.
Travelling friars and visiting monks sometimes conducted
missions or preached sermons, but these were comparatively rare events in the experience of ordinary people.
Thus ignorance and superstition multiplied. Both Word
and Sacrament had gradually been removed from the
people, and religion was in sad and grave decay. The
people remained uninstructed in the Holy Scriptures, and
in the worship they could not share. In most parish
churches even the art of singing was forgotten, and
throughout the service apart from the celebrant's occa-
sional ecphoneses only the tinkling of bells was heard.

Thus, in the centuries before the Reformation movement low mass had become the usual service in parish
churches, a service said rapidly in an unknown tongue
and in an inaudible undertone, often carried out in a
slovenly and irreverent manner. The people were encouraged to communicate only once a year, at Easter:
otherwise they could take no part. They worshipped as
spectators only, prostrating themselves in awe at the one
dramatic moment when they believed the miracle of

[1] *Liturgy and Worship*, ed. Clarke, p. 124.

transubstantiation to have taken place. It is not to be wondered at that religion became fraught with superstition, and sank into dismay.

In Scotland, too, the rural parish churches were for the most part rude small structures of rough stone, without architectural distinction, ill-kept, unheated and cold with the wind and rain beating in through unglazed windows, without much seating accommodation, floored with flags or more often with beaten earth, damp, ill-lighted, dark. Scotland in the middle ages was a relatively poor country, without, for example, the great wool trade of England, and the parish churches reflected for the most part the poverty of the people. And the poverty of the parishes was increased almost beyond belief by the alienation of the teinds to the abbeys and absentee and lay incumbents,[1] making repair and maintenance of the churches all but impossible. There were exceptions, but not many; some fine churches dating from the twelfth to the fifteenth centuries existed in some parishes, kept in repair by generous patrons; and others were well built and maintained in the burghs with their growing wealth.

By the time of the Reformation, however, a great number even of the abbeys, cathedrals, and collegiate churches had fallen into disrepair, victims of neglect, rapacity, internecine strife, and violent wars. The great period of destruction occurred not at the Reformation (for the mobs then destroyed comparatively few churches), but in the centuries preceding it when churches were often burned and robbed by pillaging invaders or their roofs destroyed for the lead by contesting nobles or kings. It was the period of hired mercenary garrisons and armies,

[1] D. Hay Fleming, *Reformation in Scotland*, p. 593, who gives many examples of this abuse. Our Norman churches, e.g., compare favourably with those of other countries. The austerity of the long gabled rectangle, representing some two-thirds of our medieval parish churches, was largely owing to alienation of parochial funds.

composed of ruthless, brutal robbers. Kirkcaldy of Grange,
writing on 1 July 1559, mentions that in Fife and an adjoin-
ing part of Perthshire the reforming rabble 'pulle doun
all maner of Freryes, and some Abayes, which willyngly
resavis not ther reformatioun', but these were in fact few
in number. Parish churches were not destroyed even by
these uncontrolled bands, but they were subjected to a
drastic and merciless 'cleansing'. 'As to Paroys churchis,
they cleyns them of ymages and all other monumentis of
ydolatrye, and commandis that no Messis be said in them;
in place therof, the Booke sett fourthe by godly Kyng
Edward is red in the same Churches.'[1] Desecration and
destruction are not, however, synonymous, and this distinction is important; nor were the reformers the first
desecrators of churches in Scotland. Comparatively few
even of the great churches were in good repair, and many
were in semi-ruin, when the Reformation movement swept
over the land.[2]

Religion and worship had all too evidently receded to
a low ebb, as a glance at the sources shows. The time
was ripe for renewal, and in Scotland that renewal came
with cataclysmic force, with revolution and rebellion;
and if the Reformation movement was late in reaching
Scotland, when it came its work was uncompromisingly
thorough.

[1] Knox, *Works*, vi, p. 33.
[2] 'While considerable mob-violence and destruction took place at the
Reformation, popular notions regarding this stand much in need of re-
orientation, for the "rascal multitude" with hammers and staves has been
invested with powers of demolition which even the modern sapper might
envy. It is conveniently forgotten that many of our ruined abbeys and
cathedrals are the result of military activity during English invasion or
civil war' (George Hay, in his invaluable article 'An Introduction to
Scottish Post-Reformation Churches' in Scot. Ecclesiological Soc.'s *Transactions*, 1951).

III

The Reformation of Worship

THE reformation of worship in Scotland was not indigenous in either its doctrinal or liturgical origins; the principles and methods that chiefly influenced it were at first English, and after 1560 Genevan.

The first service-book used in Scotland by those holding reformed opinions in the sixteenth century was the English Book of Common Prayer 1552, in the ultimate shaping of which Knox, in a sermon preached before Edward VI, had played a spectacular part by his attack upon the rubric enjoining kneeling at reception of holy communion. The Reformation was well advanced in Scotland before 1560,[1] and the reforming party had from the beginning supported an alliance with England in opposition to the 'auld alliance' with France. It was therefore a wholly natural step to use the English Prayer Book held in esteem by such leaders as John Rough, Paul Methven, Willock, and Harlaw. Even Knox at this time could 'think well of it'. His attack before Edward upon the book had produced modifications in the rubric to which he took such violent exception; and Dr. Wotherspoon rightly says,

As put into circulation and use, Edward's Second Book was so modified by Knox's influence and at his instance that, although he retained his personal objection to this and other ceremonies, he was able 'to think well of it', and to advise the congregation at Berwick, for which he counted himself

[1] See, e.g., H. J. Wotherspoon, *The Second Prayer Book of King Edward VI*, pp. 37-8; and M'Crie, *Life of John Knox*, i, pp. 159-60.

especially responsible, to yield it obedience. It represented a compromise of which he was not prepared to advise the rejection.[1]

The Book of Common Prayer was the only easily available prayer book in English at that time; but, more than that, its use in Scotland marked the unity of the Scottish reforming party with the English Protestants who had given them so much encouragement, protection, and support. The barons and nobles of the reforming party signed their first 'band' or covenant on 3 December 1557, and resolved *inter alia* that

It is thought expedient, devised, and ordeaned, that in all parochines of this Realme the Common Prayeris be read owklie on Sonnday and other festall dayis, publictlie in the Paroche Kirkis, with the Lessonis of the New and Old Testament, conform to the ordour of the Book of Common Prayeris: and of the Curattis of the parochynes be qualified, to cause thame to reid the samyn; and yf thai be nott, or yf thai refuse, that the maist qualified in the parish use and read the same.[2]

Dr. Wotherspoon somewhat pawkily remarks in his comment on the events between 1550-60 that 'Disused in the country of its origin, Edward's Second Book was in a fair way to become in natural course the rule of worship for a reformed Scotland—very much as the Directory and other Westminster Standards, so soon abandoned in their native England, have survived and are authoritative in Scotland, to which they are exotic.'[3] Such facts are worth reflecting upon in such a period as the present, when the Scottish Church is fashioning a tradition in the best sense indigenous, built out of her long history as a reformed and catholic Church.

[1] op. cit., p. 15, and Knox, *Works*, iv, p. 43; on Knox in England, see Lorimer, *John Knox and the Church of England*.
[2] Knox, *Works*, i, p. 275.   [3] op. cit., p. 41.

In the 1550s the Book of Common Prayer was so widely used that it might have looked as if it would be permanently adopted in Scotland when the Reformers gained decisive power. But this would be to forget the determinative influence of Elizabeth upon the English Reformation after she came to the throne in 1558 and the control which she exercised upon extremists. To this there was no parallel in Scotland, for the sovereign or regent did not pursue a firm policy of mediation during the critical period. Thus, as Dr. Gordon Donaldson[1] has said, 'Some divergence [from the Book of Common Prayer] was all but inevitable; not because the Scots were of a different mind from most of their English contemporaries but because they, unlike the English, had freedom to frame their services according to their own views. A preference for an order less conservative than the Book of Common Prayer was not confined to Scotland, but among Englishmen also opinion generally had by this time moved far beyond even the Second Prayer Book of Edward VI'; while in Scotland with the return of Knox opinion rapidly moved, influenced by him, towards a marked preference for the Calvinian order and forms. Nevertheless, the Book of Common Prayer continued in use in some, perhaps many, parishes until well into the 1570s.

After Knox's period as a refugee at Frankfort and Geneva during Mary's reign, and in view of the 'troubles'

---

[1] *The Making of the Scottish Prayer Book of 1637*, p. 8; this is the most recent and authoritative work on this period written with impeccable fairness and containing important new material by one with an unrivalled knowledge of the sources, and I am indebted to Dr. Donaldson for the access he allowed me to his MS. while I was preparing these lectures. See also W. M'Millan, *Worship of the Scottish Reformed Church, 1550-1638*, pp. 22 sq., a fascinating and scholarly repository of detail; and my *John Knox's Genevan Service Book*, p. 11, n. 6. Cranmer himself is said to have drafted a revision of the Book of Common Prayer, described by the Puritans as 'an hundreth tymes more perfect' (*A Brief Discourse of the Troubles begun at Frankfort in the year 1554, about the Book of Common Prayer and Ceremonies*, conveniently accessible in Arber's edition, London, 1908, p. 1).

he had had at Frankfort and the tranquil calm he enjoyed
at Geneva, it is not difficult to understand, as Dr.
Wotherspoon has said, that 'when to him almost alone
of the exiles return to England was forbidden [because
of his indiscreet and violent *Blast against the Monstrous
Regiment*[1] *of Women*], and when he turned instead to Scotland for a sphere of activity, he should have carried with
him to his native country a strong prejudice against the
Book of which he had once thought well and which he
had helped to mould, and a warm preference for the
"Order of Geneva" which he brought thither with him
as the use approved by Calvin and by the Consistory of
the city which was giving to the whole world an example
of perfected Reformation.'[2] It is important to note, however, in spite of Knox's opposition to the Book of Common
Prayer and, in particular, to kneeling at reception of
communion, that his sacramental doctrine was very high,
as Lord Eustace Percy has perspicaciously pointed out in
his erudite *John Knox*. This was evident at once in the
first Scots Confession of Faith, in the framing of which
Knox played a leading part. 'We utterly damn [con-
demn]', the Confession declares, 'the vanity of those that
affirm Sacraments to be nothing els but naked and bare
signes.' And again,

We confess and undoubtedly believe that the faithful, in
the right use of the Lord's Table, do so eat the body, and
drink the blood, of the Lord Jesus, that he remaineth in them,
and they in him; yea, they are so made flesh of his flesh,
and bone of his bone, that as the eternal Godhead hath given
to the flesh of Christ Jesus life and immortality, so doth
Christ Jesus, by his flesh and blood, eaten and drunken by
us, give unto us the same prerogatives.[3]

Chiefly influencing the Scots after 1560, however, was

---

[1] i.e., 'rule'.   [2] Wotherspoon, op. cit., p. 33.

[3] Knox, *Works*, ii, p. 185.

the reformation effected by Calvin at Geneva, and his doctrine and practice there. This reached them directly, through the writings of Calvin circulating in Scotland and through such leaders as Knox, who had been early influenced by Wishart after Wishart's return from Switzerland and who had himself lived for some years in Geneva; and indirectly in a more severe and rigid form through the English Puritans and other Anglicans.

The story,[1] therefore, begins in Strasbourg, where a Dominican monk, Diebold Schwarz, became impatient of Luther's conservative reticence in translating and reforming the mass, and determined himself to do it. This he did in 1524, and his vernacular revision was used in a celebration of holy communion in St. John's chapel, situated in a crypt north of and below the high altar in Strasbourg cathedral. This translation was further revised in successive editions, and especially under Bucer's influence after 1530; and when Calvin, driven out of Geneva because of differences with the magistrates, came to Strasbourg in 1538, he was appointed minister of the little congregation of French exiles gathered there, and permitted as a special privilege to celebrate holy communion monthly if he would agree to the Strasbourg usage. This he willingly did, and through the medium of a Latin translation, conveyed it into the terse, graceful, dignified French prose of which he was a master. And he found

[1] For details see my *John Knox's Genevan Service Book, 1556* (Edinburgh, 1931), containing texts of the Book of Common Order in the early form, and showing their derivation from Strasbourg. The complete texts of the Strasbourg liturgies are edited by F. Hubert in his *Die strassburger liturgischen Ordnungen im Zeitalter der Reformation*, Göttingen, 1900. The whole is linked with the general history of worship, and two of the Strasbourg liturgies given in translation, in my *Outline of Christian Worship* (Oxford, 1952, 5th impression). Some Scottish scholars, Professor Mitchell, H. J. Wotherspoon, John Gordon, and others, have given undue prominence to Pullain's *Liturgia Sacra* in the development of Scottish worship, an error permissible at a time when the German texts were unknown to British scholars but a position now no longer tenable.

this liturgy so much suited to his mind and taste that he took it back with him when he returned to Geneva in 1542, and with slight later alterations it became *La Forme des Prières*, Calvin's service-book in the churches of Geneva.

In 1555 John Knox, an exile from England under Mary, after various vicissitudes brought about by his objections to parts of the Book of Common Prayer,[1] came to Geneva, which he found to be 'the maist perfyt schoole of Chryst that ever was in the erth since the dayis of the Apostillis'. He became a minister of the congregation of English exiles gathered there, who worshipped in the little church of Ste. Marie la Nove, which lies across the green from the cathedral on the south side.[2] Their service-book was an English translation, with a few unimportant changes of Calvin's book, probably by Wm. Whittinghame, later Dean of Durham. Knox brought this book to Scotland (and the English Puritans carried it to England), where it passed through successive editions, and was commonly known as the Psalm-Book or Book of Common Order. It was adopted formally by the General Assembly in 1562, and first printed in Scotland by Lekprevik of Edinburgh in the same year with Psalms in metre; and an edition with the full Psalter appeared in 1564.[3] It passed through some 70 editions. Of these, one was a translation into Gaelic by John Carswell,

[1] See p. 43 supra.

[2] The church still stands, but this cradle of the Scottish (and in some respects of the English) Reformation has now become a store-room, and access to it is tedious and difficult. It is in a remarkable state of preservation, not having undergone such a succession of 'renovations' as have altered the interior of the cathedral out of all recognition from what it was in Calvin's time, and one might be allowed to wish that it could be kept open and clean.

[3] The full genealogy of this book is given in my *John Knox's Genevan Service-Book*, pp. 66 sqq.; and a list with titles of all its known editions is to be found in Wm. Cowan, *A Bibliography of the Book of Common Order and Psalm Book of the Church of Scotland, 1556-1664*, in the Papers of the Edinburgh Bibliographical Society, vol. X, Edinburgh, 1913.

printed by Lekprevik at Edinburgh, 24 April 1567. It contains an interesting form for blessing a ship on going to
sea.[1] It was also, *pace* M'Crie and others, frequently
referred to as the 'Liturgy', a word which held no terrors
for the Reformers.[2] It continued in use in Scotland until
it was supplanted by the Westminster Directory in 1645.

The Strasbourgian and Calvinian, and following these
the Scottish, reformation of worship was startlingly radical, as such considerations as the following show.

To begin with, the language used in the reformed worship was the vernacular, spoken in a strong clear voice.[3]
Thus, in one step, the ear replaced the eye. The difference
this made was profound: the congregation no longer
watched the ceremonial—which was soon reduced to
the simplest utilitarian forms, the remainder being swept
away as 'superstitious'[4]—but now listened, and hearing

---

[1] Printed in M'Crie, *Worship in Presbyterian Scotland*, p. 127.

[2] Valerand Pullain used it as the title of his service-book, '*The Holy
Liturgy*', &c. Calderwood used it: 'the liturgy or manner of the ministration of the sacraments' (*Hist.*, ii, p. 51). On 12 October 1643 the Puritan
Parliament interrupted the discussions of the Westminster Divines to order
them to take up the subject of 'the Directory of Worship or liturgy to be
hereafter used in the Church' (Lightfoot, *Journal*, p. 17); and Baillie also
speaks of 'our Scottish liturgie' (*Letters*, i, p. 226). A half-century later
that ardent pamphleteer for presbyterianism, John Anderson of Dumbarton, spoke of the 'Scotch or Genevan Liturgy' and 'our Scotch Liturgy'
(*Country Man's Letter to the Curat*, pp. 61-5). In the nineteenth century
Dr. John Cumming entitled a book, *The Liturgy of the Church of Scotland*, &c.

[3] The prototype of spoken services was low mass, said in a spoken but
almost wholly inaudible voice. The Reformers made the services audible.
But low mass itself was a radical departure from the traditional sung
service which had existed in the Church from earliest days, derived partly
but not solely from Jewish usage in which prayers, readings, and psalms
were always sung—although sung prayers are almost universal in every
religion, primitive and advanced. Psalms and hymns, we should perhaps
remind ourselves, are sung prayers. The use of music at prayer—in the
early Church even when the prayer was extemporary it was sung to traditional tones—is not formalism; its primary purpose is to do honour to
God with the voice as well as the words. And this honour may be rendered by the voice of one person as well as by the voices of many persons.

[4] What in fact was 'superstitious' was not the ceremonial itself, for ceremonial can properly be symbolical and interpretive as well as merely
utilitarian, but the popular meanings attached to many of these ceremonies.
On the whole subject, see W. H. Frere, *Religious Ceremonial*.

understood, for the words were not in Latin but in a living tongue comprehensible by all.

Further, the people were encouraged to share in the service as active participants; they were no longer passive observers. Worship became again, as it was originally, a corporate action. This popular participation was secured not only by the use of the vernacular throughout, but also by casting the psalms into metrical forms and setting them to common tunes known or easily learned by the people, tunes to which you could beat out the time and which were therefore easily sung.[1] The metrical forms too made memorizing easy, important in a period when comparatively few persons could read. Thus music, in a simple yet reverent form (as anyone will instantly recognize who seriously examines the psalm-tunes of the Reformation), was restored to the parish churches, and for the first time in centuries the voice of the people was once more heard in the praise and worship of God.[2] Except in the great churches the metrical psalms did not replace plainsong, they replaced silence.

Again, by the general adoption of the basilican posture at the holy table,[3] and in particular in Scotland by the people coming forward to sit at the communion table when receiving communion, the corporate nature of the worship as an act of the family of God was further emphasized.

Also, the Holy Scriptures were translated, and made accessible to the people. Bibles were placed in all the

[1] The strength and splendour of these early psalm tunes is evident to all familiar with them. They have recently been collected in Maurice Frost's *English and Scottish Psalm and Hymn Tunes*, c. *1543-1677*.

[2] We must not overlook the tremendous impression this made upon contemporaries; see, e.g., Erichson, *L'église française de Strasbourg*, pp. 20-4, and Herminjard, *Correspondance de Reformateurs*, i, p. 412, letter 168.

[3] The communion table has been traditionally known in Scotland as the 'holy table', e.g., the First Book of Discipline (Knox, *Works*, ii), and Burns in 'Tam o' Shanter' speaks of 'the haly table' in old Kirk-Alloway.

churches, and the Scriptures were read there daily at length, so that even those who could not read might hear.

Preaching was restored to a prominent place in worship, and the people received constant and regular instruction and exhortation out of the Holy Scriptures, on Sundays and on certain week-days alike. The sermons were normally at least one hour in length.

The old vestments with what was regarded as their superstitious symbolism were discarded, and only the clergy's out-door or preaching habit was retained—cassock, gown, hood, scarf, bands or other neckwear, cap, and gloves.

As an important step towards restoring not only the Holy Scriptures and the Word of God to the people but also worship in its Christian completeness, all the principal Reformers except Zwingli advocated weekly communion in accordance with early universal Christian practice; and in addition to frequent communion, they restored communion in both kinds. The magistrates in Geneva opposed the 'innovation' of weekly communion, unfortunately with success, and compelled Calvin against his will and convictions to accept this, though to the end of his life he contended in his writings against it.[1]

The practice in Scotland, while monthly communion was recommended in the Book of Common Order, was also less frequent communion, for both shortage of ministers and no doubt the same 'prejudice and ignorance' which Calvin refers to in Geneva prevented this reform;

[1] For details and texts see my *John Knox's Genevan Service-Book*, App. E; and Calvini *Opera*, X. i. 7, IV. xvii. 46, IV. 1051-2, II. 1047-8, X. i. 213, &c. The Reformers also reduced the sacraments, as is well known, from the traditional seven in the West to the Scriptural two, desiring to make Holy Scripture their rule in all things. 'We now, in the time of the Evangel, have two sacraments only, instituted by the Lord Jesus, and commanded to be used by all those that will be reputed members of his body—to wit, Baptism, and the Supper or Table of the Lord Jesus, called the Communion of his body and blood' (First Scots Confession, Knox, *Works*, ii, p. 185).

and it was decided that holy communion should be celebrated four times yearly in the burghs and twice yearly in the country parishes. It is unlikely that communion was in fact generally celebrated so frequently, yet the Christian duty of frequent communion was not lost sight of even in the directions of the Westminster Directory of eighty-five years later which stated that 'communion is frequently to be celebrated'. Opportunities for more frequent receiving arose out of the practice, which later became widespread, of attending the communion services of neighbouring parishes. The Reformers disputed the medieval doctrine of merit and recognized the celebration of holy communion to be a corporate action in which all the faithful should share, and in Scotland encouraged all communicants in the parish, after examination, to receive at every communion service.

The teaching of our Reformers, however, on the frequency of communion has been too long ignored by those who have come after them. The words of Dr. Sprott written some forty-five years ago are still true: 'Infrequent communion is, in my opinion, the greatest hindrance to spiritual religion which we suffer from in the Church of Scotland.'[1] To encourage frequent communion is now thought by many to be an exclusively Roman or Anglican practice. Nothing could be farther from the truth, and within modern times it was not until 1910 that the papacy began directly to advocate frequent communion of the people—400 years after the Reformers had urgently advocated it.

In the Anglican Church also, frequent communion is a recent innovation within the last century, but entirely consonant with Reformed teaching and desired by the first English Reformers. It can hardly be too much

[1] Quoted by J. Kerr, *Renascence of Worship*, p. 176; they were spoken in 1908; cf. p. 40 supra.

emphasized that the duty of frequent communion was a paramount part of the Reformers' teaching; our present general practice of infrequent communion is, as the Reformers saw clearly, a failure to embrace the full gospel.

Another point often overlooked today when Reformed worship is discussed—especially by those who write irate letters to the press about liturgies and read prayers— is the enterprising and progressive innovation of the Reformers in Strasbourg, Geneva, Zürich, England, Scotland, and nearly everywhere else, in preparing and issuing service-books for the use of the people.

Many have naïvely thought that popular use of service-books was a pre-Reformation practice, abolished by the Reformers. Precisely the reverse is true. The old Church had its service-books; but these were not at all like the modern Roman books which contain the whole service. Medieval service-books were not designed for use by the people but only by the ministers and singers who had definite functions to perform at the eucharist and other services, and each book provided only those parts of the service required by a particular minister or singer.[1] Also, the old books were in Latin, and even if the people had possessed them they would have served no useful purpose for them as few indeed were able to read or understand Latin. Further, until some forty years before the Reformation movement began in Germany, all books were copied and executed by hand, and were accordingly rare and expensive luxuries. But at the time of the Reformation, printing by the use of a press had been well developed; books were thus cheaper and more generally obtainable, and literacy gradually became more common.

In Scotland the Reformers did their utmost to establish a school in every parish, and though they were

[1] See *inter alia* Cabrol, *Books of the Latin Liturgy*, London, 1932; H. B. Swete, *Church Services and Service-Books before the Reformation*, London, 1896, 1906.

frustrated in this attempt to make the population literate, they nevertheless did all they could 'to ensure general use of the Book of Common Order. A statute required "that every minister, exhorter, and reader sall have one of the Psalm books latelie printed in Edinburgh", and in 1579 an Act of Parliament ordained "that all gentlemen with 300 marks of yearlie rent, and all substantious yeomen, etc., worth 500 pounds in lands or goods, be holden to have ane bible and psalm book". . . . Large numbers were sold. . . . The total number of editions published was seventy' between 1562 and 1644.[1]

At the Council of Trent, as part of the Counter-Reformation, the Roman service-books were reorganized, making possible the later innovation of carrying a translation of the Latin in a parallel column. But all this was a Roman reply to the success of the Reformers, who largely through the use of their service-books were able to encourage an increasing proportion of the people actively to participate in the reformed worship.

The service-book adopted at the Reformation and so long used in Scotland would not now, I suppose, be praised by anyone for its liturgical qualities, and no one would suggest it to be suitable for present-day use. It has not and would not have stood the test of time, even though it served its purpose for its day. Judged by our standards, the services were harsh and too long, the prayers too much tied to the times and on the whole lacking in a finished simple style.[2]

The metrical psalter,[3] with the exception of a few psalms, was rough and crude, and the number of tunes

[1] Millar Patrick, *Four Centuries of Scottish Psalmody*, p. 51.

[2] But that careful editing and omission can reveal a great beauty and simplicity of prose style is seen by the prayer of intercession in the first Morning Service of the Book of Common Order 1940, pp. 14-15, drawn from the old Scottish Book of Common Order.

[3] The story of Scottish metrical psalmody is told in detail by Dr. Millar Patrick in his *Four Centuries of Scottish Psalmody*.

provided small compared with contemporary Genevan or present Scottish use. Metrical psalms in several English versions had been used by those of Reformed opinions certainly as early as 1550 in Scotland, and a complete Scottish Psalter appeared in the Book of Common Order in 1564, with doxologies added a few years later. The rhyme and language were often uncouth, and the metre uneven; and while there was a considerable choice of excellent tunes, it is certain that in the greater part of the country advantage was never taken of the rich variety provided. By using common tunes (as we still do, though in greater numbers) many psalms could be sung to the same tune, and this became general practice. Also the fanatical and ruthless destruction of organs made a full musical revival impossible. Nevertheless, in the early days of the Reformation there is evidence in many parts of the country that the psalms were nobly sung, not only in unison but in parts, the 'tenor' holding the melody, and the other parts harmonizing. In 1635 a truly great Scottish Psalter was printed[1] in which the music was revised, re-allotted, and exquisitely harmonized by Millar, later Charles I's master of music. But it came too late to establish itself in Scottish worship before the period of violent differences made that impossible.

All responses were deleted from the services, except 'Amens' which were specifically enjoined in 1 Corinthians 14.16, and occurred in the Lord's Prayer and in the worship described in the book of Revelation. All other responses were much disliked by the stricter Reformers.[2] The basic reason for their dislike was in truth sacerdotal enough, as Cartwright's classical expression of it in his *Reply* of 1574 shows: 'God hath ordained the minister to this end that as in public meetings he only is the mouth

[1] Edited some years ago by Sir Richard Terry.
[2] See *Troubles at Frankfort*.

E

of the Lord from him to the people, even so he ought to be the only mouth of the people from them to the Lord, and that all the people should attend to that which is said by the minister, and in the end both declare their consent . . . and hope that it should so be and come to pass which is prayed by the word Amen.'

This view, though a perfect *non sequitur*, was still dominant a century later among the Puritans, as we see when they presented their liturgy at the Savoy Conference in 1661: 'That the repetitions and responsals of the clerk and people, and the alternate reading of the psalms and hymns, which caused a confused murmur in the congregation, may be omitted: the minister being appointed for the people in all public services appertaining unto God . . . and the people's part in public prayers to be only with silence and reverence to attend thereunto, and to declare their consent at the close, by saying Amen.'[1] All this was wholly contrary to early Christian practice, and to Jewish practice before that. Such 'clericalism' as that here affected by the Puritans would, no doubt, arouse the fiercest protests from modern objectors to responses, most of whom appear to be happily unaware of the reasons offered against their use in the sixteenth and seventeenth centuries.[2]

The omission of responses, however, was not an innovation but a continuation of contemporary practice in the Western Church, as the people had taken no responsive part in worship for centuries past, even though responses appeared in the old books. At low mass the responses were made by a server and not heard; at high or sung masses they were made not by the people but by the assisting ministers and singers; and at the offices,

---

[1] See Cardwell, *History of Conferences*, pp. 262 sqq.

[2] For the Savoy Liturgy, an interesting but hardly attractive substitute for the English Prayer-Book offered by the Puritans, see Hall, *Reliquiae Liturgicae*, IV.

they were made within the quire by the monastic company, and not by the people who, when present, occupied the nave. And, indeed, in the Book of Common Prayer, which printed the old responsive parts both in the offices and the eucharist, they were not ordinarily said by the people until some centuries later but only by the clerk, so hard did old custom die.

No lectionary appeared in the Scottish book, though the calendar[1] remained; instead of the old lectionary, which required revision, the practice was established of reading the Scriptures in course—valuable enough for daily worship but wholly unpractical for weekly worship, when we remember that there are only fifty-two Sundays in the year and accordingly seven or eight years would be required in which to read the Scriptures through. The readings (at least a chapter in length, and sometimes longer), like the sermons, we should judge to be over-long, beyond the normal person's capacity for concentration. Long exhortations were also introduced into the service of holy communion, an expansion of the old *Orate fratres* and didactic in intention. The prayers, six to eight minutes long, were not of the great length they afterwards became when men departed from the use of the Book of Common Order.

At the same time, the book presented certain proposals of enduring value which have all too easily escaped the notice of many succeeding generations. Of primary importance, for example, was the fact that it not only enjoined frequent communion but exhibited the Lord's Supper to be the normative worship of the Church. When holy communion was not celebrated, the service on Sunday mornings was still based upon and derived

---

[1] The calendar of the Book of Common Order is now being examined by Dr. Lamb, Librarian of New College, Edinburgh, and a paper by him will shortly appear in the *Records* of the Scottish History Society.

from the Lord's Supper, which in itself was a unity of word and sacrament. Great but not exclusive emphasis (as some who have come after the Reformers have erroneously maintained) was laid upon preaching and exposition of the Holy Scriptures, with a high doctrine of the Word of God.

The creeds too were considered to be central to the faith, and the Apostles' Creed was used at every service and taught in every home. The Reformers in Scotland considered this to be of first importance, as kirk-session minutes show, e.g. Glasgow 22 May 1588: 'Those who have bairns to baptize shall tell distinctly the Commands, Articles of Faith [Apostles' Creed], and Lord's Prayer, or else be declared ignorant, and some other godly person present their bairn with further punishment as the kirk thinks fit.' 20 December 1591: 'Those who are to be married declare the Ten Commandments, Articles of Faith, and Lord's Prayer, or else they shall be declared unworthy to be joined in marriage, and further censored.' 26 December 1591: 'A marriage stopped till the man learn the Ten Commandments, the Lord's Prayer, and Belief [Apostles' Creed].' 19 March 1640: 'Intimation is made by the Session that all masters of families shall give account of those in their families who hath not the Ten Commandments, Lord's Prayer, and Creed.' All these injunctions, it will be observed, belong to periods when the presbyterian party were in control.

Nor were the continental Reformers indifferent to the teaching of the Fathers—a fact which with tiresome frequency is overlooked by certain modern scholars who only too evidently have not read their works. Calvin's knowledge of patristic teaching was prodigious, and it is worth remembering, as he stated on the title-page of his service-book, that his reforms in worship were designed to reproduce primitive usage: they were 'selon l'usage de l'église primitive'. The Reformers' intention was not to innovate, but to restore faith and worship in their primitive fullness.

We may now briefly describe the Order for the Lord's Supper, which includes within it the ordinary Sunday morning service, as set out in the Book of Common Order. As we do so, it is important to note that the emphasis in the Book of Common Order is based upon the action rather than the words, and for centuries after the Reformation the Lord's Supper was commonly known in Scotland as 'the Action'. The words are often deficient as most liturgists would judge, but the four-fold action ('He took . . . , gave thanks . . . , brake . . . , and gave') stands out with much greater clarity than in Roman, Lutheran, or Anglican books, and this has always been typical of Scottish communion services.

The service began with a confession of sins, of some considerable length, followed by an extensive prayer and preceded generally in practice by a 'gathering' psalm[1] concluding with doxology[2] as with all psalms. Metrical versions were given not only of the psalms, but of the *Magnificat* 'the songe of Blessed Marie', the *Nunc dimittis*, the Apostles' Creed and the Lord's Prayer (though the prose version of both of these was normally used), the Ten Commandments, and the *Veni creator*. The doxologies, thirty-two in number, were first printed in the 1595 edition of the Book of Common Order (one in 1575) but were

[1] The phrase 'gathering' psalm derives from the fact that a Reader's service, consisting chiefly of readings from Holy Scripture, normally preceded this service. It was because of this that Scripture reading was later removed from the service proper, and when the minister came to the pulpit, he began with a psalm, and a prayer, and went directly to the sermon. People, for at least eighty years after the Reformation, were expected to be present at both services, which were a combination of the offices and the first part of the eucharist (see my *Genevan Service Book*, App. A; the development of the Scripture Readings from early practice at Strasbourg is discussed in App. B). See also p. 96 infra.

[2] M'Millan, op. cit., pp. 87 sqq.

used from the beginning.[1] The use of the Ten Commandments at the opening of the service according to Calvinian
and Anglican use was not unknown.[2] As Dr. Donaldson[3]
remarks: 'It is clear that the Scots of that period were
familiar with many things which became strange or unknown to their descendants, and that their worship had
affinities with Prayer Book services. The day was distant
when a Scottish minister would describe the Creed, the
Lord's Prayer and the Commandments as "old rotten
wheel-barrows to carry the soul to hell" ',[4] and, we may
add, think it more scandalous to sing the doxology than
a bawdy song.[5] After the confession, another psalm or
a part of a psalm may have been sung, a prayer for
illumination was said, often improvised, and the Scripture lessons followed in course from the Old and New
Testaments. Thereafter the sermon was preached. If the
alms were not collected at the church-door they were
collected now,[6] and the long prayer of thanksgiving and
intercession followed. When holy communion was not
celebrated, the Lord's Prayer and the Apostles' Creed

[1] M'Crie, *Worship in Presbyterian Scotland*, pp. 135-8; text, pp. 386-9.

[2] Sprott, op. cit., p. xxxii; M'Millan, op. cit., pp. 131-2.

[3] op. cit., p. 15.

[4] 'Jacob Curate', *Scotch Presbyterian Eloquence Displayed*, p. 21.

[5] ibid.

[6] Some twenty years or so after the Reformation in Scotland it became
common, and later normal, to collect alms at the church-door; e.g.
Glasgow Kirk-Session Minutes, 30 August 1583, 'A collector was appointed
for the first time to stand at the Laigh [Tron] Kirk door to receive alms
of Town's Folk that go into the said Kirk to hear preaching'. The Kirk-
Session Minutes of Tyninghame however show Master John Lauder, minister there from 1610 to 1662, retaining till the end of his life the old custom
of receiving the offerings at the offertory when holy communion was celebrated; on other Sundays they were taken at the church-door, and this was
also the contemporary practice at Whitekirk. Nowadays, it might be
thought strangely enough, the practice is precisely reversed in many
parishes in Scotland. What has happened is that the genuinely older
practice of receiving the offerings within the service has during the liturgical revival been generally restored on ordinary Sundays, but what is
thought to be the older practice of collecting at the door has been senti-
mentally retained on communion Sundays.

were said here; and the service ended with a psalm and the Aaronic benediction.

When holy communion was celebrated, the intercessions were followed by the Apostles' Creed, thus linking the creed with the offertory; and thereafter the elements were prepared and solemnly brought to the holy table while a psalm was sung. The minister then read the words of institution, following them with a long exhortation and the fencing of the tables. The prayer of consecration was then said, consisting of adoration, thanksgiving for creation and redemption, the anamnesis or the remembering and recalling of our Lord (and, in practice, usually an epiclesis or invocation of the Holy Spirit[1]), and a doxology, with the Lord's Prayer[2] following. Now came the

[1] The content of this prayer is truly eucharistic, and, although it contains few words and phrases of the classical liturgies, it follows the order of the early consecration prayers. The words of institution, recited not only before men but before God, were associated with the fraction. The want of an epiclesis was early felt (see Row, *History*, p. 331, quoted on p. 88 infra), and was soon supplied as Calderwood notes ('then he blessed': see description on p. 63 infra), and Henderson and Gillespie bear witness to the same effect (Sprott, op. cit., pp. xxxix-xl). The revision of 1619 contained an epiclesis (see p. 76 infra), and so did the Westminster Directory (see p. 88 infra). An epiclesis was found in the Book of Common Prayer, 1549, but was dropped in 1552; it was included in the Scottish Book of Common Prayer, 1637 (see p. 87 infra). Puritan usage in England also favoured it, as we see by the Savoy Liturgy (Hall, op. cit., iv, pp. 68, 73). It is common practice now among presbyterians the world over, as their service-books testify. There was no epiclesis in the Roman mass, but epicleses occurred in early and extra-Roman western usage and were constant in eastern usage. See my *Genevan Service Book*, pp. 134-6, for further details; and Frere, *The Consecration Prayer*, for a general history of the content of the prayer of consecration.

[2] Prof. J. M. Barkley, who has kindly obliged me with the use of the MS. of his unpublished thesis for the D.D. degree from Dublin University, 'The Eucharistic Rite in the Liturgy of the Church of Scotland', justly draws attention to an important fact: 'It will be noticed that the prayer ends with the Lord's Prayer. This was repeated by all the people. This had been the practice in the early Church, but the Roman Church had ceased to allow the people to join in this familiar prayer, and in the Roman usage it was said by the priest alone. It is sometimes thought today that the united repetition of the Lord's Prayer is an un-presbyterian thing. The reverse is more true. It was in the Presbyterian Churches that this prayer was first given back to the people' (iii. 8). He adds this word also upon the creed: 'After the Long Prayer, the Apostles' Creed, or the "Belief"

fraction, accompanied by the dominical words; and the delivery, with the minister's communion preceding that of the people.[1] During the people's communion the minister or reader might read, as directed by the rubric, 'the whole historie of the Passion', but in practice silence was often observed at this time. After communion a brief thanksgiving was said, similar to Calvin's, and a psalm (usually Psalm 103) was sung, and the people departed with the Aaronic or apostolic blessing. There were normally successive tables (and/or celebrations on successive Sundays), the people coming forward to sit at the communion tables as required.

Several contemporary accounts of a Scottish communion service exist; here we may quote Calderwood's as typical.[2] Writing about 1623, he was describing earlier

as it was called in those days, is to be repeated . . . , the basis of all instruction of the young, all the Calvinistic catechisms of those days being founded upon it. A man must be able to repeat it before he could have his child baptized, or himself be admitted to the Lord's Table, and it was regularly repeated in public worship' (iii. 9). On the continent, metrical versions of the creed were sometimes used in the Reformed congregations, but although a metrical version was provided in the Book of Common Order it is the prose version which appears to have been generally (probably exclusively) used; the same is true of the Lord's Prayer.

[1] See, e.g., Alexander Henderson's description quoted by M'Millan, op. cit., p. 173; and the details of Reformed usage given in my *Genevan Service Book*, App. F. This was universal Christian practice from earliest times: the minister, though himself unworthy, humbly set the example to Christ's people to receive the gifts their Lord gave. Modern confusion has arisen out of a misleading comparison with ordinary table manners where the host politely serves himself, or is served, last. But the minister is not the host at the Lord's Table; Christ Himself is host, and the minister like all others present a guest. It is important to keep this distinction. The minister is to set an example of humble obedience to our Lord's command by receiving what He gives, and to set the example to others he must himself receive first.

[2] *Altare Damascenum*, pp. 777-8, as translated by Sprott, *Book of Common Order*, pp. xxxviii-xxxix. There are many details of custom and practice, interesting and curious, relating to the communion services at this time: these will be found in Sprott, op. cit., M'Millan, op. cit., and A. Mitchell Hunter, *The Celebration of Communion in Scotland since the Reformation* (Scottish Church History Society *Records*, 1929, III, iii, pp. 161 sqq.); while Dr. Barkley gives a detailed account of the rite from the Reformation to the present day in his op. cit.

as well as contemporary practice; and this is his description, as translated by Dr. Sprott, of the second part of the service:

Among us, the Minister, when the sermon is finished, reads the words of institution, gives a short exhortation and admonition, then blesses. The blessing or thanksgiving ended, he says, 'Our Lord, on the night in which he was betrayed, took bread, and gave thanks, as we have already done, and brake, as I also now break, and gave to his disciples, saying (then he hands it to those nearest on the right and left), This is my Body, etc.' He adds nothing to the words of Christ, changes nothing, omits nothing. Then those next break a particle off the larger fragment or part, and hand what is left to those sitting nearest, so long as there is any portion of the fragment over. Then those who serve the Tables, when one fragment is done, offer the paten, from which another in like manner takes a similar fragment or *klasma*, and breaking, hands to the next, and so on. In like manner the Minister delivers the cup to those nearest, repeating the words of Christ, without addition, mixture, change, or omission, and they hand it to those sitting beside them; and when the wine is done, those who serve fill it anew. As soon as he has delivered both elements to those sitting nearest him, using only the words of Christ, whilst they distribute amongst themselves the bread and the cup, the Minister, as long as the action of eating and drinking lasts, addresses those at Table. . . . Whilst they are rising from the Table and others are taking their place the Minister is silent, and those leaving and those approaching the Table, together with the whole congregation either sing or the Reader reads the history of the Passion. But when the Minister is speaking and when the communicants hand to one another the elements neither is the history of the Passion read nor Psalms sung, as it is not expedient. . . . If the whole communicants could sit at one time at the Tables, it would be more agreeable and advantageous, as they could thus all together eat, drink, meditate, sing, and hear the Minister's address. . . . In this form our Church has now for sixty years celebrated the Holy Supper.

The details were not everywhere precisely the same, but the differences were slight. The elements were generally leavened bread, but sometimes a specially prepared unleavened bread or 'shortcake' was used; and wine—usually claret,[1] but sometimes other wines—as at the Last Supper, and following universal Christian usage, with water added.[2]

As mentioned earlier, the Sunday service was preceded by a reader's service, which in practice often consisted of the readings up to the confession of sins or even to the prayer for illumination before sermon.[3] Its purpose was to read the Holy Scriptures to the people, and in many places it took place daily or even twice daily, and in others on certain days of the week. Sprott's note and comment from the kirk-session records of St. Andrews, 14 August 1597, is typical of many records and descriptions: 'Mr.[4] Robert Zuill [Yule] ordained to read every day morn and even, except the days of public teaching, a chapter of the New Testament and another of the Old before noon, beginning at Genesis and Matthew, with a prayer before and after; and evening some psalms, with a prayer before and after.' Singings were also often used

[1] The quantity of wine consumed was large, even allowing for the large numbers attending; communicants were expected to do more than merely sip from the cup. As much as five gallons was ordered at a time to be brought by carrier, i.e. by pack-horse, to Whitekirk from Edinburgh (H. Waddell, *An Old Kirk Chronicle*, pp. 163-4).

[2] M'Millan, op. cit., pp. 199-208.

[3] See my *Genevan Service-Book*, Appendix A; M'Millan, op. cit., p. 136; Sprott, op. cit., pp. xxi-xxii.

[4] It may be noted in passing that the adjective 'reverend' was not in common use at this time of individual persons, but on occasion was applied to Church-courts from kirk-sessions upwards. In the late seventeenth and early eighteenth centuries it came into more general use to designate ministers. Here 'Mr.' is an abbreviation for 'Master' indicating that this Reader, probably a probationer, was a Master of Arts. Ministers then were commonly, following pre-Reformation practice, designated as 'Sir' (if not a graduate in arts), 'Master' (if a graduate), or 'Doctor' (if a D.D.), and in all ordinary address these titles were attached to their Christian names, and not to their surnames, except in some formal records or chronicles.

at the reader's service, and these were taken from the metrical psalter and the canticles.

'It is also worthy of note', says Sprott, 'that in large towns one of the churches was kept open all day for private prayers. In 1619 "the [Glasgow] Session appoints the New Kirk door to be opened from 5 in the morning and closed at 9 at night for the summer half-year, and for the winter from 7 in the morning till 5 in the evening". "This", adds Wodrow, "like the Old Kirk at Edinburgh, was for particular persons praying in the kirk." '[1] Sprott adds in the next note: 'The Session records of St. Andrew's Glasgow, and other towns, show that till 1600 the week-day sermons were preached on the old Church-days, Wednesdays and Fridays. After that date, the king directed the services to be changed to the Tuesdays (and Thursdays) to commemorate his escape from the Gowrie conspiracy.' These preaching services on week-days were common in the burghs, but were also frequent in country parishes.[2]

Communion was received sitting at the communion table, with great reverence and a deep sense of the corporateness of the act, following what was believed to be

---

[1] *Life of Weems*, p. 22; Sprott, op. cit., pp. xxxiv-xxxv.

[2] e.g., in the parish of Tynighame, Dr. Hately Waddell says of these week-day services: 'During the week there was always service every Tuesday and Friday, and preaching on both days, or preaching one day and catechizing the other. But for a long time there was daily service at eight in the morning; always reading and prayers, and often preaching as well. This was after 1638; and still in 1656, at a visitation of the church, we find the following: "Inquired anent preaching on the Lord's day, and week-day, and catechizing, ansred, That the minr. preached twise upon the Lord's day and once upon the week-day. And that he catechized once a week." The liturgical character of the reader's service was rigidly enforced; and one of the schoolmasters who, while reading the Scripture "did raise nots upon ane chapter"—that is, made a commentary upon it —was severely dealt with by the Session. As the Presbytery met on the Thursday, that day was excepted in the arrangements for daily service. In June 1644 it was enacted: "No baptisms nor marriadgis upon Thursday, seing it is a Presbitrie day, under pain of ain dolor." The service was that of the reader alone' (*An Old Kirk Chronicle*, p. 40).

apostolic practice; and long tables were placed in the church for the communicants, often arranged in T or U shape, the minister sitting at the head during communion, but standing at prayer or when addressing the people.

The services began early in the morning on Sundays, probably normally about 8 or 9 a.m., but when holy communion was celebrated as early as 3 or 4 a.m., and it was customary to receive fasting.[1] The ordinary services were about three hours in length, but when communion took place, they might be much longer, lasting far into the afternoon, depending upon the number of communicants.

Officially, the Christian year was abandoned by the Church of Scotland alone of the Reformed Churches, but there is widespread evidence that the chief dominical feasts were still kept in many places.[2] The calendar continued to be printed in successive editions in the Book of Common Order. The churches also were on occasion decorated with flowers; and with velvet, damask, or brocade hangings, save that the changing of colours to accord with the seasons of the Christian year (though there never was a fixed and absolute scheme of colours in pre-Reformation days) was abandoned because the year itself was not generally observed.[3]

Baptisms took place at the Sunday morning service 'in

[1] M'Millan, op. cit., pp. 190, 197-8. Many kirk-session records are quoted by Dr. M'Millan indicating the early hours of service. To these many more might be added, such as this record from the old Canongate Church of 5 May 1566, which is typical: 'The quilk day the commonion was ministrat according to the order [i.e., the Book of Common Order], viz. anis at four houris in the morning the uther at nyne and XI hundreth personis or thairby commonicattit, bayth the saidis services done by the minister self'; or this from Glasgow, 9 August 1589, 'The time of convening of Communion on Sundays was 4 in the morning, the collectors to assemble in the Hie Kirk [the cathedral] at 3 in the morning'.

[2] For details and sources, see Donaldson, op. cit., p. 18 n., and M'Millan, op. cit., pp. 301 sqq. Lent, for example, was a long season of abstinence from meat, which could be eaten only by licence of the Privy Council.

[3] See M'Millan, op. cit., p. 324, and also in the Church Service Society *Annual*, 1942-3, p. 16.

the face of the congregation', and if not on Sundays at one of the week-day services; and this continued for nearly sixty years, and in some parishes much longer, for private baptism was one of the innovations King James tried to effect in his much-disliked Articles of Perth. Marriages were also at first solemnized at the morning service on Sundays, and always took place in the church, for any exceptions were liable to very heavy penalties. In 1579 the General Assembly allowed them to take place on 'feriall days' at a service at which there was preaching. But so much natural merry-making was associated with weddings that kirk-sessions began to take independent action about this time, forbidding marriages on Sundays, though in many parishes they persisted until nearly the middle of the seventeenth century. But whenever they were solemnized, it was always in church. When the Westminster Directory was drawn up, the rubric advised that marriages 'be not on the Lord's Day' and forbade them on a 'day of public humiliation'. Funerals, because of the strong aversion to prayers for the departed, were preposterously 'purged': a service of any kind was absolutely forbidden at the graveside, and for a very long time none seems to have taken place anywhere; the most that was allowed were 'words of counsel' in the church before or after the interment, but no prayers.[1]

The form of worship laid down in the Book of Common Order was general in Scotland for some eighty-five years after the Reformation. The book was used as it stood by readers;[2] ministers when occasion or circumstances

[1] For the many curious customs surrounding baptisms, marriages, and funerals, see M'Millan, op. cit., pp. 266 sqq.; Sprott, op. cit., pp. xliii sqq.; for texts and notes, my *Genevan Service Book*, pp. 144 sqq. In some remote parts of Scotland communities still do not acquiesce in services at the graveside, but a service is held elsewhere, commonly at the house of the deceased.

[2] Readers were also instructed to read the English Book of Homilies (Donaldson, op. cit., p. 22).

required allowed themselves more freedom, consonant with certain rubrics in the book itself, and at one or two points in the service (particularly in the prayer before sermon) composed their own prayers, used free prayers, or prayers from the Book of Common Prayer.[1] But the intention and general practice, it must be emphasized, was not to depart from the usual prayers unless exceptional events required a change 'meet for the time'.

A considerable number of such 'composed prayers' will be found scattered through Knox's *Works*, being those he wrote for special occasions; Henderson's are with his sermons; and Principal Rollock left a collection of his prayers behind him. Prayers 'for the time' were not generally extempore during this period, but were carefully prepared for the occasion; men who believed that the Holy Spirit directed them in the preparation of their sermons did not think themselves bereft of His guidance when in their studies they prepared prayers for use in the sanctuary; and this was true also in their use of the prayers written by other godly men. An interesting series of prayers was added to the Book of Common Order in its successive editions, among them collects translated from the French, one for each psalm, which appeared in the 1595 edition —a period when presbyterians[2] were at their height of power and influence.[3]

The Book of Common Order was much more than a

[1] M'Millan, op. cit., p. 43; Donaldson, op. cit., p. 21.

[2] The words 'presbyterians' and 'episcopalians' as used here and elsewhere on succeeding pages, describe parties or persons *within* the Church of Scotland who held opposing views on ecclesiastical polity. They differed, to varying degrees, only on polity, not on points of doctrine or worship; although in the seventeenth century as the parties became more sharply defined they began to take sides also on questions of doctrine and worship. The Church, however, was not broken by organized schism until after 1690 (though some individuals went out after 1660), when various parties or groups were either excluded from the establishment or formally seceded and formed their own ecclesiastical organization.

[3] Reprinted in full by M'Crie, op. cit., App. K, and later by M'Millan in *One hundred and fifty Scots Collects*.

directory; indeed, the idea of a directory in place of a service-book was alien to the minds of the first Reformers and was a conception which grew up in Scotland in the seventeenth century chiefly owing to the influence of the more extreme English Puritans such as Browne and others. Even in 1640, the General Assembly summoned before it Raban, the Aberdeen printer, for printing only a part of one of the prayers;[1] on the other hand, such strictness of supervision did not always obtain, but varied a good deal. As Dr. Millar Patrick writes, 'The printers seem to have been allowed great latitude. When the book was published power was given to the Moderator, Ministers of Edinburgh, and the Clerk, or any three of them, to order the printing and see that the transcription for the press and the printing were well corrected. But as time went on, supervision of the work seems to have been of the most lax description. Some printers held themselves at liberty to introduce elements which had no Assembly authorization behind them.'[2] Alexander Henderson in a letter to Baillie[3] speaks of the Psalm Book 'to which ministers are to conform themselves'; clearly, however, an absolute conformity was not enforced, but deviations from it were intended to be slight and for particular reasons related to the times, as no doubt generally they were.[4] M'Crie's notion that the Book of Common Order was intended only as a 'help to the ignorant, not as a restraint upon those who could pray

[1] M'Millan, op. cit., p. 65; *Records of the Kirk*, p. 169.

[2] *Four Centuries of Scottish Psalmody*, p. 52. The same was true to a less extent of the English Prayer Book (*Donaldson*, op. cit., pp. 64, 65).

[3] Baillie's *Letters*, II, p. 2.

[4] M'Millan, op. cit., pp. 66 sqq.; Donaldson, op. cit., p. 14; Sprott, op. cit., pp. xxii-xxv. In 1624 Calderwood declares that the Church is required to maintain the order in the psalm books, which he says 'is still practised by two parts at least of the congregations of Scotland, still opponing to these innovations' (*History*, vii. 618). The 'innovations' to which he refers were those introduced by the Perth Articles six years before this (see p. 74 infra).

without a set form' is palpably absurd when you consider the massive learning of the men who first used it, e.g., Knox, Whittingehame, Coverdale, Gilby, Fox, and others, and later such men as Calderwood, Henderson, and Baillie, to name only a few.

However, the Scots Confession of Faith had stated in 1560 that one order in ceremonies could not be appointed for all ages,[1] and as early as 1584 the question of revision seems to have been raised by the King, who instructed Patrick Adamson, Archbishop of St. Andrews, to assemble the bishops and other learned men 'for taking of a uniform order to be observed in the realm in form of common prayer, and other things requisite for the good estate of the Kirk',[2] but nothing seems to have transpired. By that time English Puritan influence was beginning to make itself strongly felt in Scotland, as was evident in increasingly divergent views about worship and in controversies which, as time passed, became more bitter and extreme, though centring upon polity and vestments rather than upon worship. One revision in practice, however, seems generally to have been accepted by all schools of thought almost from the beginning, although it never appears in the book, and that is the use of an epiclesis or blessing of the elements,[3] later specifically enjoined both in the Scottish Book of Common Prayer 1637 and the Westminster Directory.

The first proposals for revision made in the courts of the Church is in 1601, that some of the prayers should be altered 'in respect they are not convenient for the time' and others deleted. The General Assembly rejected the proposals, but invited additional prayers to be

---

[1] *Confession of Faith*, chap. XX. This was also stated in the 'Declaration of Ceremonies' in the Edwardine and Elizabethan Prayer Books, and in the Thirty-nine Articles, art. 34.

[2] Calderwood, *History*, iv. p. 145.   [3] See p. 61 supra.

submitted 'meet for the time'.[1] But nothing came of it, and for several years thereafter ecclesiastical polity was the centre of interest. It was only after 1612 that King James, having secured the alterations he desired in church polity by the formation of a constitutional (to be clearly distinguished from an 'absolute') episcopacy whereby the bishops[2] worked in conjunction with the church courts, turned again to liturgical reform. Thus, as Dr. Donaldson[3] writes, 'between 1614 and 1621 we have to trace two series of measures, one concerned with the preparation of a new Scottish liturgy, and the other with the introduction of certain observances and practices which had been disused since the Reformation'.

To trace this complicated story in detail is here impossible:[4] we must select only the high lights and determinative points.

James first consulted with Archbishop Spottiswoode,[5] and afterwards, in August 1616, on the King's instructions the General Assembly 'ordained that a uniform order of liturgy, or divine service, be set down to be read

---

[1] *Book of the Universal Kirk*, ii, pp. 970-1; Sprott, *Scottish Liturgies of the Reign of James VI*, gives a year-by-year chronicle of the events. At this Assembly we may note, it was also suggested that the Bible be revised, as well as the metrical psalter; but nothing was done at that time.

[2] Three of those nominated to be bishops, Spottiswoode, Hamilton, and Lamb, were consecrated in London, their orders as presbyters being accepted as valid. Upon their return, they consecrated the remainder of those appointed to be bishops in Scotland. There was no thought at any time re-ordaining either the bishops-designate or any of the clergy. The bishops were still subject to the General Assembly for censure, and could, if needful, be deprived by the Assembly.

[3] op. cit., p. 31.

[4] The story is told in full by Dr. Donaldson in his op. cit. An earlier, but owing to missing documents less accurate, though still valuable, account of the introduction of the 1637 book is given by Professor Cooper in *The Book of Common Prayer . . . for the Use of the Church of Scotland*, Edinburgh, 1904.

[5] Sprott, *Scottish Liturgies . . . James VI*, pp. xvi-xvii, prints Spottiswoode's memorandum, which covers revision of the services, a new Confession of Faith 'so near as can be with the Confession of the English Church', orders for electing bishops and ministers, new forms for the sacraments, marriage, confirmation, etc., and new 'canons and constitutions'.

in all kirks', and set up a committee of four[1] to 'revise the Book of Common Prayers contained in the Psalm Book, and to set down a common form of ordinary service to be used in all time hereafter' by ministers and readers.[2]

A reason given for this desire to have a set liturgy, a contemporary tract[3] states, was 'the deformity which was used in Scotland, where no set or public form of prayer was used, but preachers, or readers, and ignorant school-masters prayed in the church, sometimes so ignorantly as it was a shame to all religion to have the majesty of God so barbarously spoken unto, sometimes so seditiously that their prayers were plain libels'. The authorship of this tract, published in the name of Charles I and written in 1639, is attributed to Dr. W. Balcanqual, then Dean of Durham; we need not be surprised therefore to find some inaccuracies and exaggerations. The statement that 'no set or public form of prayer was used' is quite untrue, as the evidence of such men as Brereton, Henderson, Gillespie, and others before-quoted proves; the second part of the statement is liable also to exaggeration, but there is no doubt that 'some', but a minority at this time, did out-rageously misuse and extend the freedom allowed in the way the Declaration describes, even to the point of foster-ing sedition.[4] It was in view of such possible excesses that Calvin many years before this had written to Somerset, 'I highly approve of it that there should be a certain form from which the ministers be not allowed to vary: that first, some provision be made to help the unskilfulness

[1] Patrick Galloway, Peter Ewat (or Hewat), John Adamson, and William Erskine, not by any means 'king's men'; see Sprott, op. cit., p. xxiv.

[2] *B.U.K.*, iii, pp. 1123, 1128, 1132.

[3] *A Large Declaration concerning the late Tumults in Scotland*, p. 16.

[4] See p. 140 infra; and the case of Hog, who prayed against bishops as 'bellygods and hirelings', recorded in Calderwood, *History*, vii, pp. 368-9. Contemporary records show very plainly that there were some to whom restraint in such matters was an unknown quality, and it was a habit which persisted and increased in later times.

and simplicity of some; secondly, that the consent and harmony of the Churches one with another may appear; and lastly, that the capricious giddiness and levity of such as effect innovations may be prevented'.[1]

The work of the committee was to be examined by a larger commission of bishops and ministers to meet in Edinburgh in December. The draft they drew up is well known as Hewat's or Howat's draft, edited by Dr. Sprott.[2] In general order it conformed closely to the structure familiar in the Book of Common Order, but fixed prose psalms were introduced, with gospels and epistles (this order is probably a misprint) to be read in course; prayers were increased in length, and the prayer after sermon contained more detail than formerly, while prayers and phrases from the Book of Common Prayer were woven in together with many of the prayers in the Book of Common Order, which were allowed still to be used as they stood. The draft deals only with divine service, as instructed; the remainder of the Book of Common Order was unchanged. Howat, an Edinburgh minister, was a man of moderate views,[3] but very critical of later innovations; his draft therefore not only witnesses to a general desire for liturgical reform, but also is interesting as an example of what moderate men could then agree upon.

However, the King was presently busy chiefly with getting more complete control of the Church; and, visiting Scotland, was intent upon restoring the principal festivals of the liturgical year. He began by ordering all ministers to celebrate holy communion at Easter, and was at work upon a code of canons.

---

[1] *Opera*, xiii, p. 70.

[2] Contained in his *Scottish Liturgies of the Reign of James VI*; the period of James's and Charles's reign is covered by Dr. Sprott in his introduction.

[3] Spottiswoode, however, who obviously had no great respect for him, describes him as one who 'loved ever to be meddling, and was always set to make trouble' (*History*, iii, p. 244).

Before his visit, James ordered the Chapel Royal at Holy-rood to be refitted, and an organ, stalls for choristers, and statues of the apostles and evangelists, to be placed in it. The 'images' alarmed the populace, and several of the bishops and clergy wrote to the king to dissuade him from carrying out this part of his plan. He was very angry, but yielded, not, he told them, for the ease of their minds, or to confirm them in their errors, but because the statues could not be got ready in time. On the 13th May he re-entered Scotland, after nearly 14 years' absence. On the 17th the English service was read in the Chapel Royal 'with singing of choristers, surplices, and playing on organs'; and on Whitsunday, June 8th, the Lord's Supper was administered after the English form, by an English clergyman, and was generally received kneeling.[1]

This was followed by an angry controversy about the freedom of the Church, raised by the King's persuading the Scottish Parliament to pass an Act to the effect that 'whatever conclusion taken by his Majesty . . . should have the power and strength of an ecclesiastical law'. The year 1617 drew thus to a stormy close.

In 1618, the famous Articles of Perth[2] appeared, enjoining kneeling to receive holy communion, private communion for the sick, private baptism when circumstances required it, confirmation, and the due observance of Christmas, Good Friday, Easter, and Whitsun. These articles aroused bitter opposition, and divided the Church into sharply-defined contending parties, because James's reforms, which hitherto had chiefly effected the clergy, now for the first time touched the laity at a very tender

[1] Sprott, op. cit., p. xvii.

[2] These were passed at the King's instruction by an Assembly composed as far as possible of persons who would be amenable to doing as the King wished, but it was not accomplished without heated debate. Lord Binning was a King's Commissioner at this Assembly; Thomas Hamilton of Priestfield, King's Advocate, he had been created Lord Binning in 1613, Earl of Melrose in 1619, and in 1619 resigned that title and 'changed his style to Haddington, not choosing to have his title from a Kirk living'.

point; and kneeling at the reception of holy communion in especial provoked widespread indignation and resentment. M'Millan's estimate of the position[1] is a fair and sagacious summing up, and worth recording anew:

The greatest change, or at least the change which caused the greatest trouble in the period 1560-1638, in the ritual of the Scottish Communion Service was that which introduced kneeling instead of sitting at the reception of the elements. Nothing that king James ever did in ecclesiastical matters in his northern kingdom, neither his banishment of popular ministers, nor his introduction of episcopacy, aroused greater antagonism than his determination to make Scottish communicants receive the Bread and Wine 'humbly kneeling' at the Communion Table. The other four Articles of Perth were harmless in comparison to this. It was easily the most obnoxious, since it suggested in the most vivid way the ceremonial of the Mass, which Scots remembered had been regarded by Knox as more to be feared than armed enemies. Indeed, it is probably not too much to say that the later troubles would not have arisen if James, and after him Charles, had allowed the people to keep what they believed to be the posture of Christ, who, on the night in which He was betrayed, sat down with the Twelve.

Meantime, efforts were being made to achieve closer liturgical uniformity with England, and the work of revision proceeded, continued by a commission of the Perth Assembly, Howat and Erskine no longer taking part but being replaced by men more ready to comply with the King's wishes. Eventually, a second draft—a

---

[1] op. cit., p. 178. See also Sprott, who is of the same opinion in his op. cit., p. xxxiii: 'To one article, that of kneeling at the Communion, the strongest objection was felt, and the change of posture had the effect of bringing the laity into action, and of placing a great part of the nation in direct opposition to the King. The people had been accustomed to kneel at the prayers in the Communion Service [Lindsay's *True Narrative of the Perth Assembly*, p. 47, says, "We were accustomed to kneel at the thanksgiving", i.e., the prayer of consecration.], but kneeling in the act of receiving they regarded as savouring of idolatry.'

complete prayer-book—was compiled. Associated with
the name of William Cowper, Bishop of Galloway, who
died in February 1619, it must have been finished soon
after the Perth Assembly, and probably represents the
work of the two previous years between the Aberdeen and
Perth Assemblies.[1] Archbishop Spottiswoode sent it to
the King, who with Young, the Scots Dean of Winchester,
made certain alterations, and on 30 June 1619 Gilbert
Dick was licensed to print the book. While more advanced
than the former draft, it was a genuine compromise, and
the structure of the Book of Common Order was still
respected and reasonable choice provided in the prayers.

If feelings had not been running high because of what
had recently passed and the Five Articles in particular,
it might have had a chance of being considered on its
merits. But that was not now possible. Laud kept press-
ing the King to go farther, but James whose boast it was
—and not without foundation—that he knew 'the stomach'
of his Scots people, would have none of it. Indeed, the
King decided to drop, for the present at any rate, his
liturgical revision, and a promise was given in his name
to Parliament by the Marquis of Hamilton and Archbishop Spottiswoode that if they ratified the Five Articles,
that would be an end of innovations. Parliament accordingly by a vote of seventy-five to fifty-one did as the King
desired. The liturgical reforms which were so promising
and in themselves had roused little hostility, were given
up for the sake of the Five Articles, which were in truth
worth little. Beyond ordering that the Book of Common
Prayer should be used, at least in part, in some cathedrals,
in the university chapels, and in the royal chapel, liturgical revision stopped till James's death in 1625, and was
not revived by Charles till 1629. With Charles a new

[1] See text in Sprott, *Scottish Liturgies*, pp. 25 sqq., and Donaldson, op.
cit., pp. 36-38.

and fateful chapter began, and thirteen years scarce had passed before the structure James had painfully and skilfully reared tumbled into ruins.[1]

[1] At this point, words of Professor Cooper deserve to be recalled to our recollection: 'The blow struck in 1637 had enduring consequences. All that the wisdom, by no means inconsiderable, of King James VI, all that the piety, the munificence, the taste of his son had desired for the Church of Scotland, was henceforth discredited in the eyes of the vast bulk of the Scottish people, and its realization postponed indefinitely. That union and communion between the two national Churches, which the different circumstances of their respective Reformations had not availed to break, suffered now an interruption which has not yet been terminated. . . . The difficulty created by those unhappy proceedings still stands in the way' (op. cit., x). And he concludes by quoting lines from the *Veni Creator* in the version used in the fateful book of 1637:

> Of all strife and confusion,
>   O Lord, dissolve the bands:
> And make the knots of peace and love
>   Throughout all Christian lands.

IV

Worship and the Covenants

CHARLES began with a policy of conciliation and moderation, for in 1626, a year after he ascended the throne, he instructed the Scottish bishops not to enforce the Articles of Perth upon any minister ordained before 1618 who had scruples against them.[1] They, on their part, were not to speak in public against them, dissuade others from obeying them, or refuse communion to those who wished to receive kneeling. But it was an intrinsically unworkable compromise, even if feelings and prejudices had not already been inflamed by this and other controversies, for it could never really have satisfied those in opposition or healed the deep differences now dividing the Church. And if it had succeeded in satisfying the ministers, it would still have left the people unsatisfied, for congregations and parishes were also sharply divided by these controversies, in particular the controversy over kneeling at communion. It was this no doubt that led the ministers of Edinburgh two years later to ask to be allowed to celebrate without requiring the communicants to kneel, in an effort to keep peace within their parishes. The King, it may be understandably but still unwisely offended, refused; and confusion resulted.[2]

[1] Balfour, *Annals*, ii, pp. 142-5. M'Crie ignores this, and much else, in his *Public Worship in Presbyterian Scotland*.

[2] Row, *History*, p. 348; Stevenson, *History*, p. 115; see M'Millan, op. cit., pp. 182-3. Nevertheless, after Charles's coronation in Scotland (on 18 June 1633) kneeling seems to have become common; and by 1636 was customary in Edinburgh and the north but was opposed in the southwest (*Early Travellers in Scotland* (1635), pp. 147, 159; A. Cant in *Memorials*, ii, p. 185).

There were difficulties too about the minister communicating each person individually instead of using the
method favoured by the first Scottish Reformers derived
from the Last Supper of allowing the communicants to
pass the elements from hand to hand, the minister serving
only those persons immediately to his right and left.[1]

Charles just at this time also roused the bitter enmity
of a great body of Scottish landowners by his settlement
of the teinds derived from old Church lands in 1627,[2]
but he does not appear to have received much gratitude
and loyalty from many of the ministers whose royal
champion and benefactor he was.

Laud became Bishop of London in 1628, and in 1629
the King raised the question of liturgical revision in Scotland; and John Maxwell, a minister of Edinburgh and
later Bishop of Ross, took the draft south for the King's
information. But both the King and Laud desired Scotland to adopt the English Book of Common Prayer 'that
so the same service book might be established in all his
majesty's dominions'.[3] In brief, Laud's policy as chief

[1] See, e.g., M'Millan, op. cit., pp. 184 sqq.

[2] *Acts of the Parliaments of Scotland*, v, pp. 189-207, 218-19; Cook, ii, pp.
330-2; Napier, *Montrose and the Covenanters*, pp. 78-91. Hume Brown
declares this just settlement to have been one of 'the two main causes for
the revolt of 1638', the other being the new service-book; and of the two
it (the Act of Revocation) receives the most 'emphatic illustration in the
proceedings of the Privy Council of Scotland' (in his Introduction of the
Register of the Privy Council of Scotland, III. p. ix). The lairds and nobility
saw in rebellion against the King's authority a golden opportunity to
resume their alienation of teinds and lands.

[3] Laud's *History of his Troubles and Trial*; the whole passage is quoted in
Sprott, *Scottish Liturgies*, pp. xliv-xlv. In the paper of instructions which
Balcanqual used to compile the King's *Declaration*, there is this statement:
'To facilitate the receiving of the Book of Common Prayer, a care was had
besides to make it as perfect as could be, so likewise that howsoever it
should come as near to this of England as could be, yet it should be in
something different, that our Church and kingdom might not grumble
as though we were a Church dependent from or subordinate to them'
(ibid., p. xliii). Sprott (op. cit., pp. xli-lvi) and Donaldson (op. cit., pp.
41-59) both give in much more detail than is here necessary or possible
the narrative of this period, with excerpts from the relevant sources.

adviser to the King was from the beginning to have a
prayer-book common to Scotland and England; and, by
so doing, he would have a powerful lever also to insure
greater conformity to the Book of Common Prayer in
England. Success in Scotland would have enabled him
more effectively, or so he thought, to beat down Puritan
opposition in England. Allowance for this fact must
always be made in our judgement of Charles; he was
King of both England and Scotland. Maxwell, however,
continued strongly to urge that the Scottish people would
be much better satisfied if a liturgy were framed by their
own clergy than 'to have the English liturgy put upon
them'.

There the matter stood for four years, and nothing
more occurred till Charles came to Scotland for coronation,[1] accompanied by Laud, when he required the English Prayer Book to be used at the services he attended.
Shortly afterwards, the first edition in Scotland of the
English Prayer Book was published, two more editions
following in the next year (1634); and the King required
it to be used in the cathedrals, universities, and Chapel
Royal.

We may pause a moment here to glance at the arrangements in the quire of the Chapel Royal as described in
a contemporary document:

In time of service within the Chapel, the organist and all
the singing men are in black gowns, the boys in sad coloured
coats, and the usher, the sexton, and the vestry keeper are
in brown gowns. The singing men do sit in seats, lately
made, before the noblemen, and the boys before them, with
their books laid as in your majesty's chapel here [London].
One of the great Bibles is placed in the middle of the Chapel
for the reader, the other before the dean. There is sung

---

[1] For accounts of the coronation, see Balfour, *Annals*, ii, pp. 193-8;
Rushworth, *Historical Collections*, ii, p. 182; Spalding Club, *Mem. of the
Troubles*, i, pp. 36-7.

before sermon a full anthem, and after the sermon an anthem alone in versus with the organ.[1]

The day after the coronation in 1633 the Scottish Parliament had resolved (by a doubtful vote) to continue to Charles the power granted to James to regulate ecclesiastical dress. There was opposition among the clergy to this Act; but nevertheless Charles in conformity with it instructed Ballantine, Bishop of Dunblane and Dean of the Chapel Royal, in October of that year to preach 'in his whites' and enjoined that copes be worn at celebrations of the Lord's Supper in the Chapel. By a warrant, the bishops were directed always to wear 'a rochet and sleeves' in church, and at meetings of the privy council and court of session. 'A chymer, that is, a satin or taffeta gown without lining or sleeves' was 'to be worn over their whites at the time of their consecration'. Ministers were to preach in black gowns, but to wear surplices when reading the prayers, administering sacraments, and burying the dead.[2] At that time ministers wore black gowns, cassock, &c.,[3] at all services and at the General Assembly, and continued to do so till 1638, when for the first time many appeared in Glasgow in ordinary clothes and armed.

Meantime, in May 1634, Charles had given the Scottish bishops his consent to prepare their own service-book; and Bishop Maxwell, sent south later in the year for precise directions from the King, returned with a copy of the Book of Common Prayer signed by Charles on 28 September, containing alterations, instructions, and

---

[1] See Grub, *Ecclesiastical History of Scotland*, ii, p. 347.

[2] Stevenson, *History*, p. 144; *Acts of Parliament*, v, p. 21.

[3] Beadles, too, commonly wore a gown or 'cloak', with 'shoon', for use in the church and church-yard, and carried a 'staff' or 'wand' not merely as a token of authority but for the very practical business of 'crubbing of bairns' and keeping order generally. This apparel and accoutrement was provided by the kirk-session, and had long been customary.

suggestions.[1] The changes were slight: the communion service was untouched, the doxology added to the Lord's Prayer, the Authorized Version used in several places, 'priest' was preferred to 'minister', and some freedom was allowed in keeping of holy days.

The Authorized Version was ultimately used in the 1637 book in all passages, including the psalms, taken from Holy Scripture. 'There were other reasons besides the excellence of the version which helped to recommend it. It could not but be more agreeable than any purely *English* version to the Scots, who boasted that the first suggestion of it had been made in the General Assembly of their Church at Burntisland [1601] prior to the union of the Crowns, and that the work appeared under the authority of their native-born prince; while to Charles himself it at once harmonized with his general policy and gratified his filial affection.'[2] The use of the Authorized Version was meant no doubt partly as a concession to Scottish wishes, but in fact it had not at this time been much taken up in Scotland, and it was never officially authorized here. The first Scottish edition was issued in 1633, printed by Young, printer also of the 1637 prayer-book. Since the Reformation the Geneva Bible had been generally used in Scotland; the Authorized Version was not cordially received and was used but little before 1645, the Geneva Bible continuing in use in some parishes until the end of the eighteenth century.[3]

'On the whole, the changes expressed in this [the 1634] book show every sign of having emanated from the King personally, and seem to reflect the views of a somewhat

[1] This book, formerly believed lost, was recently discovered by the Earl of Haddington in his library; it has now been collated with the 1637 book by Dr. Donaldson in his op. cit.

[2] Cooper, *Book of Common Prayer 1637*, p. xvi.

[3] See Principal Lee, *Memorial for Bible Society*, pp. 112-13.

small-minded and sacerdotally-inclined layman, rather than of a churchman interested in doctrine and other larger issues.'[1] With it came instructions to frame the new book 'with all convenient diligence, and that as near as can be to this of England', and meantime to report progress to Laud. Diligence was shown, and within a year, in September 1635, printing began by the King's command; but the book was never issued,[2] for more radical counsels now prevailed among the Scottish bishops. The younger bishops gained the ascendancy, and Wedder-burn[3] urged that 'if they did not then make the book as perfect as they could, they should never be able to get it perfected after'.

Discussion was now focused upon the communion service, and the desire of the Scottish bishops was to bring it into conformity with classical Christian usage by altering and completing the prayer of consecration, specifically directing the manual acts following Scottish and general, but not Anglican, custom of the period, and omitting the second sentence in the words of administration. It has sometimes been said that the Scots objected to the removal of this explanatory second clause added to the words of administration in 1552, but I have never seen the evidence quoted, and it is unlikely that the matter ever received any particular consideration from them except as an afterthought. They had always been accustomed at this point to using the words of Holy Scripture, and would probably have disliked any doctrinal additions to it. The proposed formula of the 1637 book was not stronger in any sense than the words later used in the Westminster Directory,

[1] Donaldson, op. cit., p. 47.

[2] Baillie, *Letters*, i, p. 4, says 'much of it was printed'.

[3] Dean of the Chapel Royal and nominated to the see of Dunblane in February 1636, he was a descendant of an old Scottish Reforming family, 'a man of antique probity and faith, and for his excellent learning a great ornament to his fatherland' (see Cooper, op. cit., pp. xviii-xix).

'Take ye, eat ye, this is the Body of Christ which was broken for you; this do in remembrance of him'.

A copy of the Book of Common Prayer with the alterations allowed written in by Laud was signed by the King on 19 April 1636, and the volume is still to be found in Christ Church Library, Oxford.[1]

About this time also the King by royal authority and without consulting the General Assembly or Parliament imposed upon the Church the Book of Canons. These really 'did away with the Kirk-Session and the Presbytery . . . and thus would have swept away the Ministry of Discipline as established by the standards of 1560 and 1578'.[2] This aroused the keen resentment of those opposed to episcopacy and among many not urgently concerned about previous controversies, and helped to increase and harden the opposition. The canons were declared null by the Glasgow Assembly in 1638.

Laud wrote to Wedderburn on 20 April, and 'it is beyond doubt that the initiative in suggesting all the significant changes in the Communion Office—concerned not with trivialities of ornaments or posture or phraseology, but with points of fundamental eucharistic doctrine —had come from Scotland and that the substance of the Scottish demands had been approved'.[3]

A few more changes were made, including the tidying up of the rubrics, the insertion of 'or sung' where often 'said' only occurred, and by express royal command the addition of some lessons from the Apocrypha (carefully secreted by the Scottish bishops among saints' days and

---

[1] The text is included in Dr. Donaldson's study; and the letter accompanying it, written by Laud, is printed in full in Cooper, op. cit., pp. xxviii-xxxii.

[2] I. M. Clark, *A History of Church Discipline in Scotland*, p. 122.

[3] Donaldson, op. cit., p. 53. 'To Bishop Wedderburn of Dunblane, it would seem, most of the liturgical features which characterize this service-book were due' (Cooper, op. cit., p. xviii).

lesser feasts not observed in Scotland). The use of the Apocrypha was now much opposed in Scotland by the majority, and as only the Old and New Testaments were prescribed after the Reformation, it was probably never used much, if at all. Nevertheless, it is interesting to remark that the Apocryphal books were contained in the Geneva Bible of 1560, evidently being thought worthy of printing and inclusion even though a note in the preface stated that they 'were not received by common consent to be read and expounded publicly in the Church'. On the title-page itself the Old and New Testaments only are mentioned.

The King now signed the warrant in which he said, 'I gave the Archbishop of Canterbury command to make the alterations expressed in this book, and to fit a liturgy for the Church of Scotland'. This was the sentence that gave gross offence; what followed was scarcely read, for the injunction continues, 'And wheresoever they shall differ from another booke signed by me at Hampton Court, Sept. 28, 1634, our pleasure is to have these followed rather than the former unless the Abp. of St. Andrews and his brethren shall see apparent reason to the contrary. At Whitehall, April 19, 1636.'[1] The King had not, in fact, at the time given the instruction so specifically to the Archbishop of Canterbury, for as we have seen the Scottish bishops played a principal part in the preparation of the book. The King's statement was used against Laud later, but 'it is noticeable that contemporaries were less unanimous than their posterity in attributing the book to Laud. Baillie stated that "Dr. Coosings is thought the main penner of our Scottish Liturgie".[2] Some of his fellow-countrymen, however, did not even look south of the border for its authorization. The National Petition against the service-book said, "The

[1] See Cooper, op. cit., pp. xxxii and liii.   [2] Letters, i, p. 226.

archbishops and bishops of this realm have drawn up and set furth" the book.'[1]

It came from the press in May 1637, and the Privy Council commanded its use in the churches. Neither the General Assembly nor Parliament was consulted; and beyond a few of the bishops those who were to use it had never seen it in its final form.[2]

The book was first read in the churches on Sunday 23 July 1637. In St. Giles' Cathedral, Edinburgh, it was introduced after the prayers from the Book of Common Order had been read for the last time, as the dean sadly remarked and believed; and a furious riot broke out both inside and outside the church, and similarly in other Edinburgh churches, notably Greyfriars. The rioting was far from spontaneous, and had been carefully organized.[3] From that day, and indeed from long before, the book was doomed. Remonstrances, many of them dignified but all of them firm, were sent up from many presbyteries and kirk-sessions; and at the Glasgow Assembly next year it was swept away, and the episcopate with it, and the National Covenant was widely embraced. But not by all; the Covenant was strongly resisted in Aberdeen and the north, and the Aberdeen Doctors wrote learnedly and vehemently against it; and in many other places it had to be forced upon the inhabitants 'at the sword's point'.[4]

To discuss the details wherein the book was a concession to Scottish wishes, and the uneasy and perilous path Charles had to tread in not conceding too much

[1] Donaldson, op. cit., p. 79.

[2] Baillie, *Letters*, i, pp. 4, 16, 31. Who was responsible for this unconstitutional and foolish action it is not now possible to say; the King took the action, but upon whose advice? or did he act without advice? In any event, the result was fatal to his plans and hopes (see Donaldson, op. cit., pp. 78-83, and Cooper, op. cit., p. xxii for a fuller discussion).

[3] Spalding, *History of Troubles*, i, pp. 46-8; Guthrie, *Memoirs*, pp. 20-1; Henderson, *An Advertisement* in Scottish History *Records*, xxiii.

[4] Scott, *Legend of Montrose*.

lest he weaken his position with the Puritans in England, is not here necessary, for in a sense it does not matter as all minds were made up. The objections made against the book were a 'cover' for deeper resentments, and therefore on the whole were not reasoned but emotional and at times hysterical; and the pamphlets against the book, even those written by eminent and scholarly men, betray this on every page. The objections—when there was any serious attempt to argue them—were all borrowed from English Puritanism; none was an independent Scottish view; they had all been stated eighty years before in England against the Book of Common Prayer.[1]

The objectors disliked responses,[2] favoured excessively long detailed prayers, and hated the apt brevity of the collects. One even finds Row, who a little before had complained of its omission, now complaining against the inclusion of the epiclesis. An epiclesis or an invocation of the Holy Spirit was included later in the Westminster Directory, and Calderwood, Henderson, Gillespie, and Spottiswoode, among others, mention it as a typical Scottish usage.[3] It was never an English usage, for it disappeared from the Book of Common Prayer, not to return

[1] Conveniently summarized with quoted sources by Professor Horton Davies, in his *Worship of the English Puritans* (1948), especially pp. 57 sqq. One point, however, as Dr. Barkley points out, should be made clear. There is a misunderstanding 'common among Anglicans, and sometimes taken up and repeated by Presbyterians. The Anglican scholar compares the "Liturgy of 1637" with the English Prayer Book of the time, from his point of view, and considers it much "higher". He then remarks on the stupidity of Charles and Laud in trying to force upon the Church of Scotland, not merely the "Book of Common Prayer, 1552" but actually a more high Church version of it. Such an outlook does a grave injustice to Laud. The Book of Common Prayer 1549 was altered in 1552. Some of the alterations may have been in a more Puritan direction, but others were towards Zwinglianism (Dix, *Shape of Liturgy*, pp. 656, 659, 668), and so were as offensive to a Calvinist as to a Romanist. It may be safely said that there is not one difference between the Book of Common Prayer 1552 and the Liturgy of 1637 which would have made the latter more objectionable to Presbyterians than the former' (op. cit., ch. iii, p. 28).

[2] See pp. 55-56 supra.   [3] See p. 61 supra.

G

till the secularly rejected but ecclesiastically permitted book of 1928. Row, writing in 1622, after relating the episode of a communion table being overturned and a cup spilled owing to the communicants having knelt at reception, says, 'Mr. Patrick Galloway haveing kneeled and prayed, I would say, having read the prayer of consecration, wherein there is not one word of Lord bless the elements or action . . .'.[1] But when he venomously criticizes the 1637 book his complaint is reversed: 'It hath the verie popish consecration, that the Lord would sanctifie, by his word and holie Spirit "those creatures of bread and wine that they may be unto us the bodie and blood of his Son".'[2] Row must have known perfectly well that there was no epiclesis in the Roman consecration prayer, and if he did not know, so much the worse of him; his criticism is either wilfully or ignorantly unjust. Nor do the words of which he complains differ essentially from the directions of the Westminster Directory later: 'Earnestly to pray to God to vouchsafe his gracious presence, and the effectual working of his Spirit in us; and so to sanctify these Elements both of Bread and Wine . . . that we may receive by faith the Body and Blood of Jesus Christ, crucified for us, and so to feed upon him, that he may be one with us, and we with him; that he may live in us, and we in him, and to him who hath loved us, and given himself for us . . .'. It is of course present Scottish usage.[3]

The more extreme section of the opposition, to Baillie's high indignation, were soon to attack even the Lord's Prayer, and the doxology. Baillie complains in 1643 of some Ayrshire ministers who had drawn up a paper in 'a very bitter and arrogant strain against the three innocent

---

[1] *History*, p. 331.   [2] ibid., p. 339.

[3] See the Book of Common Order 1940; on general Christian usage, see Atchley, *On the Epiclesis of the Eucharistic Liturgy*.

ceremonies, Paternoster, Gloria Patri, and kneeling in the pulpit, proving by a great rabble of arguments . . . the unlawfulness of our Church practices'.[1] He says Henderson, Rutherford, and others, had agreed to write replies for 'quenching of the fire', and 'expressed themselves passionately against these conceits'. And Dr. Sprott reminds us that 'the Commission of the covenanting Assembly of 1642, Robert Douglas, Moderator, threatened with deposition some ministers in the south and west who had given up these laudable customs'.[2] We are all familiar with the tradition of Calderwood's famous appeal in the General Assembly of 1649, when it was proposed to drop the doxology at the end of the psalms: 'Moderator, I entreat that the doxology be not laid aside, for I hope to sing it in heaven.'[3] But although his plea was successful then, this and 'other distinctive usages, on which the older Scottish churchmen set much value', had in the end 'to be sacrificed to the prejudices of the extremer Puritans' and their sympathizers in Scotland. The less extreme Puritans, as we see by the Savoy Liturgy, objected not to the use of the doxology, but to its excessively frequent (as they believed) repetition.

Some of these old distinctive usages were gradually omitted by tacit concurrence, such as 'the saying of the Apostles' Creed by sponsors, and the singing of the ascription of glory to the Holy Trinity at the end of the Psalms. The Scottish Assembly openly required that the minister's private devotions in the pulpit, before beginning service, should be discontinued, as a concession to the English. And though the Lord's Prayer and lessons of Scripture were enjoined in the Directory, they soon followed the other "nocent ceremonies" [the same that Baillie had

[1] *Letters*, ii, pp. 69-71.   [2] *Worship and Offices*, p. 19.

[3] Kerr, *Renascence of Worship*, p. 1; see also M'Crie, *Worship in Presbyterian Scotland*, pp. 205, 210-18.

called "innocent ceremonies"], and were hardly ever heard in our churches for 200 years.'[1] The extreme objectors, it must be said, had no understanding whatever of what common worship should be as an action in which the whole Christian family actively shares.

Following the repudiation of the 1637 book, and the expulsion of the bishops by the Assembly in 1638, worship appears to have continued for a time much as before; but the tempest and chaos had a hardening effect upon men's minds, and fostered a rapid increase in Puritan extremism.

This is evident in a revealing extract, quoted by Dr. Sprott, from Wodrow's MS. 'Life of Ramsay' (University of Glasgow Library); it is an account of a paper written by Alexander Ramsay, a covenanter and moderator of the Aberdeen Assembly of 1640, against the innovations introduced by some since 1638. Ramsay

instances leaving off of the Lord's Prayer at the end of public prayers, as had been usual formerly, and though Christ had prescribed it, and it is most perfect, yet not one in a hundred uses it. It was the practice formerly to use forms of prayer, as also extemporary prayers, before and after sermon; now extemporary prayers only were used. This, says Mr. Ramsay, is not agreeable to many places of the Word of God. . . . He thinks the vast difference pretended by the enemies of forms between prayer flowing from the Spirit and forms says much for forms, because those are much more adapted to the words of the Spirit in Scripture than extemporary prayers are. Forms may be easier joined with than unpremeditated effusions, and they are less subject to errors and mistakes. Another novelty, he reckons, is the disuse of prayer by persons alone in churches. . . . The Temple was built not only for joint prayer, but that single persons might come and put up their particular petitions suitable to their cases. Again, he says, of late all public reading of the Scriptures in the

[1] Leishman, *Westminster Directory*, p. xviii.

Church is laid aside as dry and useless unless there be a Minister to explain it. . . . The profession of the Creed in Baptism is laid aside, though very anciently used in the Christian Church . . . and godfathers in Baptism are laid aside, to the hurt both of parents and of children when they come of age. He complains that the long custom that Ministers, when they enter the pulpit, before they preach to the people, address themselves to God for his Spirit promised and given, is abrogat, to the great loss both of Ministers and people.[1]

Several editions of the Book of Common Order appeared—the printer Raban at Aberdeen, to whom we earlier referred, was during this period rebuked for his unauthorized changes—but it is doubtful if it was so consistently followed as in former days. The evidence, as we have seen, is conflicting. But the veneration in which many held the book is reflected in the correspondence between Baillie and Henderson in 1642, when a revision was proposed, and Henderson gave as one of his reasons for not proceeding with it, 'nor could I take it upon me . . . to set down other forms of prayer than we have in our Psalm-book, penned by our great and divine Reformers'.[2] Baillie too was uneasy in his mind about the likely results, for later he confided to Henderson his view that 'the Directory might serve many good ends, but no ways for suppressing, but much increasing the ill of novations'.[3] The moderate men desired as strongly to repel unauthorized Puritan innovations as they did those proposed by the King.

The National Covenant of 1638 was followed in 1643 by the Solemn League and Covenant sanctioned by the Assembly and Estates in August. In contrast to the National Covenant it was an oppressive and fanatical document in which the Scottish subscribers banded themselves

[1] Sprott, *Book of Common Order*, p. xxxi.
[2] Baillie, *Letters*, ii, p. 2.   [3] ibid., ii, p. 95.

together with the English parliamentarians (while oddly still professing their loyalty to the King) to secure their presbyterian polity and worship as binding upon the three Churches of England, Ireland, and Scotland. Just as Charles and Laud had worked to bring these three countries into a greater and firmer unity by uniting them under one ecclesiastical polity and worship, episcopacy and the Prayer Book; so now the parties to the Solemn League and Covenant in the so-called defence of their liberties in fact pledged themselves by force of arms and with an even more intolerant spirit to impose their favoured polity and worship upon these same three countries, for they also believed that ecclesiastical unity was essential to a true civil unity.

Accordingly, to the Westminster Assembly of Divines which met in 1643 was given the task of drawing up an agreed Confession of Faith, Directory of Public Worship, and scheme of ecclesiastical polity. It consisted largely of English clergy (many of whom did not attend), some Members of Parliament, ten or eleven Independents, and a handful of Scots clergy and laymen who came as assessors with the right to speak and debate but not to vote. Nowadays we should describe such an assembly as a parliamentary commission. 'Its members had been nominated by the English Parliament, with many of their own numbers included. Its work was prescribed and limited, its president and rules of procedure appointed by the same authority. Parliament did not hesitate to dictate the order in which they should carry on their business, to hurry them when they seemed dilatory, and to review and alter their decisions at pleasure.'[1] The Scots, though invited by Parliament, were nominated by the General Assembly. Parliament at this time was acting without and against the authority of the King. The

[1] Leishman, op. cit., p. x.

Assembly of Divines completed the Directory in 1644.

Before we describe the worship set forth in the West-minster Directory, for purposes of easy comparison let us glance back at the form of worship common in Scotland during the previous thirty or forty years. It is described by William Cowper,[1] Minister at Perth 1595-1612 and Bishop of Galloway 1612-19, Sir William Brereton,[2] an English Puritan visiting Scotland in 1635, and Alexander Henderson,[3] the well-known, trusted, and learned Coven-anter who was Moderator of the Glasgow 1638 Assembly, writing in 1641. These three accounts, written by men of widely differing schools of thought and ecclesiastical practice, differ but very minutely in detail and agree in the main structure of the worship; and this in itself is interesting testimony to the general unanimity of prac-tice during this period. In addition to these we have the Book of Common Order itself, mention of various cus-toms in contemporary letters and ecclesiastical records, and the directions in the Books of Discipline. The dif-ferences, however, are in the main slight and a general picture is easy to paint; though we are to bear in mind that worship during this period was not absolutely uni-form; there were local customs and habits, and Dr. William M'Millan deals with the plenitude of these.[4] Besides this, there were variations on small points: the choice and number of psalms sung in a service, the quality of the music, the choice and length of the passages read from Holy Scripture, and the amount of extempore, set, or composed prayer used.

We are also to remind ourselves that for eighty years or more after the Reformation, and especially in the

[1] In *Seven-days Conference between a Catholic Christian and a Catholic Roman*, contained in Cowper's *Works*, p. 639.

[2] In Hume Brown, *Early Travellers in Scotland*, p. 147.

[3] In *The Government and Order of the Church of Scotland* (1641).

[4] *Worship in the Scottish Reformed Church, 1550-1638*.

early period, there were large numbers of readers in Scotland and, for a short time, exhorters. These were at first drawn chiefly from the many former clerks in orders, not judged qualified to be ministers. Of ministers there were at first few, but their numbers gradually increased.[1] This meant that in more than two-thirds of the parishes to begin with, and for some considerable time afterwards, services were of necessity conducted by readers only; and in some, later many, parishes there were both a minister and a reader. Where there was only a reader, he was instructed to use the Book of Common Order without varying from it, and to read homilies from the English Book of Homilies.[2] Where there was a minister as well as a reader, it was normal practice for the reader to conduct the first part of the service; during the 'reader's service' the minister was usually absent, not going to the church until he went into the pulpit after the readings were ended. The reader conducted his part of the service from the lectern or 'lateron', which was usually the lower deck of a two-decker pulpit, and he normally acted also as precentor; the minister conducted his service from the pulpit.

Calvinian and Strasbourgian practice, following early Christian usage, had been to conduct worship from the communion table, which was left in the chancel or sanctuary but moved out a little from the east wall so that the minister could take up the basilican posture; and when holy communion was celebrated, the people came forward and stood at the holy table to receive, being given the bread at one end of the table and the wine at the other, two ministers serving. In Scotland, the method

[1] In 1567, for about 1080 churches there were 455 readers, 151 exhorters, and 257 ministers; seven years later, for about 988 churches, there were 715 readers, no exhorters, and 289 ministers (see the convenient summary of the position in M'Crie's notes in Appendix A, pp. 428 sqq. of *The Public Worship of Presbyterian Scotland*).

[2] See p. 67 supra.

adopted when holy communion was celebrated was to place tables in the sanctuary or in the body of the church at which the people sat to receive communion; on the Sundays when there was no communion, the tables were removed. Consequently, in Scotland the minister conducted his service from the pulpit; but now that the method of receiving communion has been altered[1] and communion tables are continuously in the churches, they should be treated as the focal point of Christian worship in conformity with universal Christian practice from earliest times and all worship should be led from them.[2]

Turning to the details of the service, our narrators inform us that the people were called to assemble for worship by the ringing of the first bell about half an hour before the service began; at the next bell, rung at 8 or 9 o'clock, the reader began his service. He commonly read the confession of sins in the Book of Common Order, then led the people in a psalm or psalms in metre each concluding with the doxology, read a chapter or chapters in course out of both the Old and New Testaments, possibly with further psalms or canticles sung between them. This service continued, says Brereton, 'till about 10 hours'; and Cowper says 'these exercises are used in all our congregations every Sabbath[3] one hour before the preacher

[1] See p. 171 infra.

[2] For details of early Reformed practice, see my *John Knox's Genevan Service-Book*, pp. 36 sqq.

[3] It is interesting to see the bishop using the word 'Sabbath'; the early Reformers seem generally to have preferred 'the Lord's Day'. It is noticeable in kirk-session Minutes that 'Sunday' and 'Lord's day' predominate till about 1640, after which 'Sabbath' gains, but never holds the field. In the early period after the Reformation the Sabbath seems generally to have been held to begin at daybreak on Sunday morning; e.g., cf. this minute from the Glasgow kirk-session, 17 January 1590: 'The brethren interpret the Sabbath to be from sun to sun, no work to be done between light and light in winter, and between sun and sun in summer.' But in the 1640s this is changed: 18 August 1640, 'The brethren declare the Sabbath to be from 12 on Saturday night to 12 on Sunday night.' The same holds of Tyninghame.

comes in'. At about 10 o'clock the third bell rang, and
the minister entered the pulpit as a psalm was being
sung. 'The psalm being ended', the Puritan traveller
says, the minister 'reads a printed and prescribed prayer,
which is an excellent prayer', while the bishop says that
at this point the minister 'conceives a prayer'.[1] It is
interesting to find the Puritan praising the prescribed
prayer, and the bishop mentioning with approval the
extemporary prayer. The practice itself varied, but 'conceived prayer' at this time was often and probably usually
prepared beforehand with a special purpose in view,[2] and
the Book of Common Order allowed it at this point.
The minister next read a text from Holy Scripture, and
preached his sermon upon it; though some with Puritan
views had added another psalm here and followed it by
an intercessory prayer before sermon; or sometimes they
attached the intercessions to the conceived prayer. The
conceived prayer was ordinarily a prayer for illumination before sermon, and the addition of another prayer
was a Puritan disturbance of the logical and traditional
order; and Baillie quite properly deplored this. The sermon was an hour or more in length; and it was followed
by a long prayer of thanksgiving and intercession, the
thanksgiving was linked with the heads of the sermon
and the intercessions for all men united the congregation
with all Christ's faithful people. It concluded with the
Lord's Prayer and the Apostles' Creed. Then the people
sang another psalm, after which 'the minister blesseth
the people in the name of the Lord, and so demits them'.

This service lasted till about 12 noon, being some two
hours or more in length. If there was no minister, the
sermon was of necessity omitted but homilies were often

[1] During this prayer we are told that 'the people humble themselves',
i.e. kneel. Cowper, *Works*, p. 639.

[2] See pp. 67-70 supra.

substituted, and the readings lasted longer; there was possibly more singing, and the reader read the prescribed prayers from the Book of Common Order. The attitude at prayer everywhere was kneeling,[1] on both knees or on one knee; hats were removed for prayers, psalms, and readings, but were usually though not always worn during sermon by the preacher and the men,[2] and the women wore plaids or shawls on their heads, and in many places sat separate from the men.[3]

'Andrew Ramsay, moderator of the Aberdeen Assembly of 1640, writing some years later, mentions among the "innovations" which had been introduced into the Church since 1638 the omission of the Lord's Prayer in public worship.[4] Burnet in his *Vindication of the Church of Scotland*,[5] writing of the period 1638-45, speaks of the disuse of the Lord's Prayer, and says that the General Assembly took this in very ill part. Baillie blames the Brownists for this, alleging that they taught the people to "scunner" at both the Lord's Prayer and the Belief.'[6] About this time too began the voluble habit in some places of 'lecturing', expounding Scripture instead of reading it, a practice Baillie observed with no favour. 'If all this', he

---

[1] See, e.g., M'Crie, *Worship in Presbyterian Scotland*, p. 150: 'kneeling in public worship had been practised in Scotland among Presbyterians from the time of the Reformation. Thus . . . in [21 June] 1587 the Glasgow Session ordained "that all persons in time of prayer bow their knee to the ground" ' (Wodrow, *Weems*, 22). See M'Millan, op. cit., p. 151, for other examples, and my *Genevan Service-Book*, App. D, for early Reformed practice.

[2] 'In that you may do as your health requires' says Cowper; but it was not governed so much by health as by general custom going back into pre-Reformation times.

[3] Glasgow 10 July 1589, 'The session ordains that no woman sit upon or occupy the forms the men should sit on, but either sit laigh [i.e., on the floor] or els bring stools wi' them'. Forty-eight years later Jenny Geddes (?) obediently brought her stool with her, but allowed it to be put to more aggressive use, and this indeed was not the last time stools were used as weapons in church, as records of this and the succeeding century show.

[4] See p. 90 supra.   [5] Sage, *Fundamental Charter*, p. 356.

[6] M'Millan, op. cit., pp. 130-1.

said, 'be laid on the minister before he preach, we fear it put preaching in a more narrow and discreditable roume than we would wish.'[1] He also wrote in strong terms to his colleagues at the Westminster Assembly concerning the desire of the Independents to abolish the reader's office and with it the reading of the Holy Scriptures in church. (The Puritans had objected of old to the reading of the Scriptures at public worship, unless expounded as they were read. Cox, writing in 1573 of the more extreme Puritans, said, 'They cannot endure the reading of Holy Scripture in the church'.)[2] If we agree to this, wrote Baillie, 'we put down that exercise of public prayer in all our towns, we cast out all our readers as unlawful officers, we lay a very heavy burden on the most of our ministers; besides twice preaching, catechizing, baptizing, marrying, and holding a session, we will have him to pray, sing, read, both before and after noon'.[3] His gloomy prophecy about the abolition of public daily prayers and the casting out of readers was sadly and amply fulfilled within a few years.[4]

To understand the setting of this worship, we require to glance at the Reformers' use of the old churches. By the time of the Reformation, as observed in a previous chapter, owing to internal strife and invading armies as well as to neglect by many of the incumbents and the alienation of teinds, most of the parish churches were in disrepair, and many also of the abbey, cathedral, burgh, and collegiate churches had severely suffered. Efforts were made by the Reformers to put them into good if somewhat uncouth repair, but their funds were limited,

---

[1] *Letters*, ii, p. 122.   [2] *Zürich Letters*, i, p. 281.

[3] His complete memorandum is reprinted in Leishman, *Westminster Directory*, pp. 189-91. It should be said that kirk-sessions normally met before service every Sunday, and often several times each week, to deal with discipline; and presbyteries met weekly. This was general under both presbytery and episcopacy.

[4] See p. 107 infra.

and much of the work was makeshift and rude. Thus during much of the seventeenth and eighteenth centuries the medieval church-buildings remained uninviting, dismal, cold places. Apart from some great churches[1] and burgh churches, the old buildings were usually small, narrow, dark, and dank, rectangular in shape, with earthen floors, still often disturbed for burials leaving bones scattered about and a settled and prevailing odour of the dead. The roofs were, more often that not, thatched with heather or turf in the medieval manner, as in former times (straw was much too valuable and scarce to be used for roofing), the walls decayed, the windows small, and dampness was everywhere prevalent, increased by the raised level of the ground in the churchyards where burials had taken place for centuries. Through the roofs, the rain trickled in, to make it damper still. In 1690, the heritors were urgently charged with maintaining the churches in repair, but in a period when a laird's annual income was about £50, such admonitions had little effect.

Generally speaking, stools and backless benches distributed about the church served as seats, and the orderly arrangement of chairs or pews as we know them and the box pews which preceded them, did not come in till the eighteenth and nineteenth centuries. But after the Reformation there was a general effort to provide seating accommodation more commodious than formerly,[2]

[1] The cathedrals and great churches, if they could be used as parish churches were usually so adapted and used by the Reformers, and kept in such repair as funds allowed of. For details, see C. A. Ralegh Radford and G. Donaldson, 'The Post-Reformation Church at Whithorn', in the *Proceedings of the Society of Antiquaries of Scotland*, lxxxv, Session 1950-1; and, more extensively, Geo. Hay in Scot. Eccl. Soc.'s *Transactions*, 1951.

[2] What happened in Glasgow on 25 April 1588 occurred elsewhere also, when the session appointed 'some ash trees in the Hie Kirk [the cathedral] Yard to be cut down to make forms for the folk to sit on in the Kirk'. In 1560 the town council ordered 'sattis, furmes, and stullis' for the High Kirk [St. Giles'] of Edinburgh; and in 1639 decided that all the burgh churches should have 'pews or desks'. More examples could be given.

and kirk-session records bear ample witness that these sometimes served as clubs and missiles to settle brawls amid cries and oaths before service began.[1] The lairds and corporations had their pews or lofts, often of fine design and craftsmanship enriched with carving and colour, some with canopies. In the eighteenth century, heritors had to provide seating for two-thirds 'of the examinable persons of the parish', i.e., those over twelve years of age.

To adapt the old churches for Reformed worship a wall often replaced the quire or chancel screen, and side-aisles were sometimes walled off; the disused chancels were allowed to fall into ruins or to become burying-places. Some of the larger churches, as St. Giles' in Edinburgh, were divided into two or three churches by walls.

A few churches were built during this time. An example is Burntisland, in 1592, where a square design of some merit was preferred, with the pulpit commanding the whole, and the central part of the church available for the tables when holy communion was celebrated. In the early seventeenth century, some semi-ruinous churches, such as Melrose and Dunfermline Abbeys, were put in a state of repair, and the plan forms of new churches were the rectangle, the T-plan, and the Greek cross, in that order of number and importance, such as Greyfriars in Edinburgh, Dirleton, Old Cumnock, Dairsie, Ayr, Careston, South Queensferry, Anstruther Easter, Largo, and Pittenweem.[2]   A few more churches were built

[1] Behaviour in church was far from decorous during this period, and indeed till well into the eighteenth century, as records show. In Glasgow, e.g., on 20 June 1644 'The session directs that the Magistrates shall attend the Tables at the Communion in the Hie Kirk, and keep order.' Keeping order was also no small part of the beadle's duties.

[2] Further details in Radford and Donaldson, pp. 127-8; and for the best comprehensive account of Scottish churches (though it is not always wholly accurate in view of later study), see M'Gibbon and Ross, *Ecclesiastical Architecture in Scotland*, 3 vols. Most valuable and accurate for this period is Geo. Hay in Scot. Eccl. Soc.'s *Transactions*, 1951.

towards the end of the seventeenth century, the Canongate in Edinburgh being a fine example, recently so effectively renovated. It was only in the last quarter of the eighteenth century, and continuing on after that, that many new Scottish churches were built, as the medieval churches sufficed till then. In the sixteenth and seventeenth centuries, many fine pulpits were constructed, in Germany, Belgium, Holland, Denmark, Sweden, and indeed in other parts of Europe in both Roman and Reformed churches. The Scottish pulpits of this period were often richly carved and generally of good design, but on the whole simpler than the opulent and splendid erections so frequently seen still on the continent; all, of course, both here and abroad had sounding-boards or testers. Unfortunately in Scotland most of these pulpits have now ceased to exist through neglect or because they were considered by 'restoring' vandals to be out-of-fashion; and even where the pulpits remain, the testers have often been removed and destroyed by ruthless and misguided men. Thus does our heritage perish, as in some places it is still perishing because ministers, kirk-sessions, and presbyteries will not trouble to learn what they should preserve or to value what they possess. Most of these pulpits were double-deckers, with the minister above and the reader or precentor below. So far as I can recollect, none now remains in its original condition (though some have been partly restored),[1] and we must look at rare old prints and paintings or visit other countries to see what they were like.

[1] One has been completely restored, surrounded by its lower enclosure, by Mr. Ian Lindsay in the old parish church at Ayr, and it well illustrates the dignity and beauty of the Scottish pulpits of this period. There is also a good example in St. Salvator's Chapel in St. Andrews (the University chapel). The 'latteron' or 'lower deck' still remains, but the tester has unfortunately gone. A similar pulpit, much restored, once belonging to the Barony church, now stands in the quire of Glasgow cathedral, but both lower desk and tester have disappeared. Further good examples are in Kirkcudbright, Spott, Gifford, Pencaitland, Bo'ness, Elgin, &c.

Let us now turn to the worship framed by the extensive and detailed rubrics which define the service so minutely in the Westminster Directory. The chief architects of this, as I have said, were clergy of the Church of England, mostly but not wholly of presbyterian or Puritan opinions, assisted by a small group of Independents and Scottish assessors. In it we see the influence of both the Book of Common Prayer and the Book of Common Order, and often the relationship is verbal as well as structural. It represents an amalgam and a compromise. It was adopted by the General Assembly in 1645, and is still a standard of worship in the Church of Scotland, with the explicit proviso stated in the Act of Assembly, 3 February 1645, Sess. 10, that approval of the Directory should 'be no prejudice to the order and practice of this Kirk'.[1] In it the reader's and minister's service were combined; or, looked at from the Anglican side, matins and ante-communion were compressed together with all responses omitted. The office of reader began to disappear, and his service went with him.

The Sunday service of the Directory was to open with a dignified summons to worship, followed by a prayer of approach to God, consisting of adoration, a supplication for worthiness to stand before God, and prayer for illumination of the Holy Scripture. Then a chapter from each Testament was to be read in course, and metrical psalms might be sung or prose psalms read before or between or following the readings.

If he so desired, the minister was permitted to lecture at this point, i.e., 'to expound any part of what is read'. Careful safeguards were introduced in the hope (a vain one!) that this practice would not be abused: 'let it not be done until the whole Chapter or Psalm be ended; and regard is always to be had unto the time, that neither

[1] Printed in full in Leishman, op. cit., App. B.

Preaching, or other Ordinance be straitened, or rendered tedious. Which rule is to be observed in all other public performances.' The permission was abused—and for nearly two centuries—but lecturing was finally denounced by the General Assembly in 1856, when it enjoined that all ministers 'observe the recommendations . . . respecting the *reading* of the Holy Scriptures in the Directory'.[1]

Next came a confession of sins, of which the details are set out at great length, prayer for pardon and absolution and for a sanctified life. (Joined to this, following English Puritan usage, was the prayer of intercession, but the Scots were determined to follow their own custom, and in Scotland provision was made for the intercessions to be included in the prayer after sermon.)

The sermon followed, after which came the general prayer. It consisted of thanksgiving, especially for the gospel and redemption; supplications related to the heads of the sermon; self-oblation, and a petition that the spiritual sacrifice of worship should be acceptable to God. Then, in Scotland, general intercessions were offered, for the whole world, the Reformed and British Churches, the King, Queen, and all in authority, pastors, teachers, schools, universities, city or town, parish and congregation, all in distress; for seasonable weather and fruitful seasons; special prayers suited to the times; prayer for the sanctification of the Lord's day, grace to enter into fuller fellowship with God; and for the minister in his office and life. Then the Lord's Prayer was said, and sometimes also, following old Scottish use, the Apostles' Creed which was printed in the Catechisms and required to be learned by all.

English Independent influence secured the omission of the creed against Scottish wishes: 'the Apostles' Creed they detest' wrote Baillie (*Dissuasive*, 30), 'as an old

---

[1] Leishman, op. cit., p. xxxi.

H

Patchery of evil stuff.' The omission was evidently noted by Parliament, for the Westminster Assembly on 16 December 1644 instructed Dr. Burges to inform the House 'that the reason why the Assembly have sent up nothing in the Directory, concerning the Creed and the Ten Commandments, is because they reserve it for . . . catechizing, where they conceive it will be most proper'.[1]

If there was no celebration of holy communion, the service concluded at this point with a psalm of praise, and the solemn blessing of the people by the minister.

When holy communion was celebrated, the closing psalm became the offertory psalm, during which the holy table was decently covered, and the sacred elements brought in and placed upon it 'before the Minister'. It is not clear whether the minister was intended to take part in the procession of the elements or not, but it appears that in practice he normally did. A long exhortation followed as a preparation for communion, and the tables were formally and solemnly fenced. The elements were then set apart from all common uses, the words of institution read from 1 Corinthians, and a very long exhortation followed upon this. Now the prayer of consecration was offered,[2] consisting of a prayer for access, thanksgiving for creation and providence, redemption, and the word and sacraments, then the anamnesis or 'the memorial of our Lord' and epiclesis or invocation of the Holy Spirit, followed by the Lord's Prayer. Next came the fraction with the dominical words; and after that the delivery and communion, the celebrant receiving first

[1] Mitchell and Struthers, *Minutes*, p. 21.

[2] At the Westminster Assembly the correct posture during the prayer of consecration was discussed. Henderson explained the Scottish practice at this time: 'The Table is full, the Minister comes, reads the words of institution, and prays standing; and the people either sit or kneel at prayer-time indifferently, but are sure to sit in the act of receiving' (Lightfoot, *Works*, xiii, p. 296).

according to universal Christian custom. When all had received, the minister exhorted the people to a worthy life, and the post-communion prayer was said in which thanks were given for the benefits of holy communion, and petition made for a better way of life. A psalm was then sung, and the people were dismissed with a solemn blessing.

The directions both for the Sunday service and for holy communion are generously comprehensive, and there would have been no difficulty in filling up three hours on ordinary Sundays and many more at the communion, had they been followed in every detail. But it seems unlikely, with few exceptions, that they were ever closely followed. The Act of Assembly (3 February 1645, Sess. 10) was specific enough:

Doth unanimously, and without a contrary voice, agree to and approve the following Directory, in all the heads thereof, and the intent of the Preface, it be carefully and uniformly observed and practised by all the ministers and others within this Kingdom whom it doth concern; which practice shall be begun, upon intimation given to the several Presbyteries from the Commissioners of this General Assembly, who shall also take special care for timeous printing of this Directory, that a printed copy of it be provided and kept for the use of every kirk in this Kingdom; also that each Presbytery have a printed copy thereof for their use, and take special notice of the observation or neglect thereof in every congregation within their bounds, and make known the same to the Provincial or General Assembly, as there shall be cause.

In England the Directory won little favour, but it was held by many as being within its intention to be used liturgically, and Leishman prints an example of this use.[1]

Attempts seem to have been made in some of the presbyteries in Scotland to carry out the injunction of

[1] op. cit., App. D.

the General Assembly: the Presbytery of Ayr enacted in August 1645:[1]

The Directory in its principal parts is ordered to be read in all the churches on Sabbath eight-days, and on the Lord's day thereafter to be uniformly practised by the whole brethren.

Mention of it is also made in the *Life of John Row*:[2]

The 2 of November 1645—The which day I read in effect the Directory of Public Worshipping of God to our people, and that with great trouble, being to teach again at afternoon. . . . The 29 of March 1646—I began this day to practise the order set down in the Directory for public Worship; for my son, Mr. Robert Row, had practised it in this Kirk the Sabbath before, and besought me to essay it, because many thought that I had been against that good order.

The Directory was issued, we must remember, in a period of turmoil, when there was much division and contention in the Church; most ministers therefore ignored the Directory, continuing in their own ways; and at the Restoration, Parliament annulled the Act which introduced it. English Puritan opinions, as we have seen, were also gaining ground and worship became barer still.

Thus, the doxology began to be omitted after the psalms; and even the metrical psalms fell into disuse in many places, as in Edinburgh where their use ceased for several years. 'In 1645 within the Synod of Lothian, the reading of Scriptures, and the singing of psalms were "discharged" from the people's worship, and in place of them came in "lectures by ministers, which continued till the incoming of the English Army".'[3] Psalmody was in fact restored only in 1658, and the reading of Scripture in 1661 at the beginning of the second Episcopacy, at

---

[1] Edgar, *Old Church Life in Scotland*, series I, Lecture ii, p. 60.

[2] Woodrow Society, pp. xxxi, xxxii.

[3] Millar Patrick, op. cit., p. 107.

which time also the doxology was ordered to be sung as
formerly at the end of each metrical psalm. Tedious 'lecturing' replaced the reading of the Holy Scriptures; long,
detailed, exhaustive, and exhausting extemporary prayers
increasingly became the fashion of the times; the Apostles'
Creed and Lord's Prayer fell into increasing disuse. The
abolition of the readers at this time resulted, as Baillie
had warned, in the suppression of daily prayers. For
three or four years the ministers in Edinburgh, for example, had daily prayers with exposition, but they soon
tired of it,[1] and no doubt the people tired of it too.

About 1640 we begin also to notice a new emphasis
on family prayers which gradually replace the week-day
prayers in the parish church; and at the same time the
week-day services shift their emphasis from prayer to
preaching and catechizing. A minute of the kirk-session
of Glasgow, for example, enjoins on 19 March 1640 that
all members of households must know the Ten Commandments, Lord's Prayer, and Apostles' Creed, and
adds 'That every family shall have prayers and psalms,
morning and evening', and that 'some of the fittest men
shall assist the elders in promoting this work'. In January
of that year the same movement is seen in the east, for
at Tyninghame the minister now began to 'schew to the
pepill out of the pulpitt the necessity of familie exerceise,
and exhortit the pepill thairto'. Thereafter, exhortations
to family worship are frequent, and the daily service
gradually disappears. On 30 September 1649, we have
this stated in the records:

The minister earnestlie exhortit the elders to observe and
continewe constantlie Familie Exerceise, and publicklie in
his doctrin, and intimat yit again as often befor to the pepill
to observe the same, and that he was to come to particular

[1] Wodrow, *Analecta*, pp. 290, 368.

families and ane elder or twa of everie pairt of the parische with him to sie if it wer done, utherwayis he wald proceid against the neglecters thairof according to order.

And there is this note:

Item, the minister schew to the sessioun that my Lord Hadinton's familie had Familie Exerceise twyse everie day preceislie keipit, and catecheising in the familie twyse in the week to the gude exampil of the rest, and, thairfor desyrit the elders to hold haud to the same.

To further this, the General Assembly had 'Buiks of privat worship and mutual edification' published, and Master John, the minister, succeeded in selling 'threttie copies' of them within the parish.

Fasts were also introduced before holy communion— a great innovation, for fasts hitherto had been related not to holy communion but to national and local discipline or calamities. 'The Ordour and Doctrine of the General Faste' was issued in 1566, and included in the Book of Common Order in 1587; it was a discipline enjoined for times of special trial. It was normally divided into two parts: the 'abstinence' and the 'humiliation'. The 'abstinence' began on Saturday night, lasting till after the afternoon service on Sunday; and the 'humiliation', a period of special penitence, meditation, and prayer, began on the Sunday morning, lasting for a week. The Sunday might be preceded by special preparation on the Saturday, or, in the country, on the Sunday before the fast began. Appropriate services of some three hours' length in the morning and two hours in the afternoon were held on the Sundays, and on week-days two services of one hour each were held. On certain rare occasions, a celebration of the Lord's Supper was linked with the fast, as in Edinburgh in 1566, and 1574, and in St. Andrews in 1572; and similarly in Newcastle in 1584 by the exiled

James Melville and his friends.[1] The purpose of introducing communion at this time was to heighten the solemnity of the fast.[2] But during the Cromwellian period, the
fast began to be associated with the communion by the
Protesters as a preparation for communion;[3] and after
the Revolution, when the Protesters became the dominant
party in the Church this became the general and established custom, to last for nearly two centuries, and in the
north not wholly absent from our practice yet.

During Cromwell's time also another new custom grew
up, originating with the Protesters and fostered by them;
and it too established itself in general custom after the
Revolution, and continued, though after 1750 in reduced
numbers and modified form, for a very considerable
period. This was the new custom of having great crowds
and many preachers at holy communion, developing into
a habit of several parishes uniting for these services.

A pamphlet of 1657 describes it:

Our dissenting brethren [i.e., the Protesters] have taken up
a new and irregular way. To omit their way of admitting
persons who come from other congregations, they do not now
usually celebrate that ordinance but they have a great many
ministers gathered unto it, six or seven, and sometimes double
or more, whose congregations most part are left destitute of
preaching that day; a great confluence from all the country,

---

[1] See M'Millan, op. cit., pp. 330-3; and Sprott, *Book of Common Order*, p. l.

[2] In Glasgow in 1595, however, a fast day at communion was introduced
to heighten the solemnity of the communion season: 'A fast day is to be
kept for both days of the communion [i.e. on the two consecutive Sundays—an innovation indeed, for Sunday had never been observed as a
fast day in times past] that the Lord's day be not profaned by pastimes
and plays'; and the magistrates forbade games and plays 'to be used in
the Town for two weeks before Communion'.

[3] Glasgow, 1655: the session enacted that 'the fast is to be on the Thursday before the Communion. There are to be sermons on Saturday and
Monday at the three kirks, and on Sunday at the Blackfriars, to such as
will repair thither. The doors will not be open on Sunday till 6 in the
morning.'

and many congregations about, are gathered at them; and on every day of their meeting, which are Saturday, the Lord's day, and Monday, many of these ministers do preach successively one after another; so that three or four, and sometimes more, do preach at their preparation, and as many on the Monday following. And on the Lord's day sometimes three or four preach before they go to the Action, besides those who preach to the multitude of people that cannot be contained in the church.[1]

During this period also, as we have seen, metrical psalmody grievously declined, and even fell into disuse in many parishes after 1645.[2] To remedy this regression, a new version of the psalms, based upon Rous's but radically revised, was issued in 1650, and that metrical psalter is still in use today.[3] Rugged and craggy though it may be, it was more graceful in its versification than the old versions, and possessed of a masculinity of style which gave it enduring qualities. It was also limited in the number and variety of its metres, and this provided greater opportunity for the use of common tunes and made a gradual revival of psalmody possible. The revival was, however, long-delayed; for it was stultified for nearly two hundred years by the introduction at this time from England of the revolting practice of 'lining', which, while it endured, made any real recovery impossible. 'Lining' was the practice of the precentor reading, or singing in a monotone or according to some private method of his own, one line of a metrical psalm, after which the people sang that line as near to the tune specified as they could get (and this was often not recognizably near it); and so throughout the psalm or the portion of the psalm selected for this treatment. The practice grew out of the need to

[1] *A True Representation*, &c., quoted by Leishman in Story, *Church of Scotland*, v., pp. 390-1.

[2] See Millar Patrick, *Four Centuries of Scottish Psalmody*.

[3] On the whole, see Millar Patrick, op. cit,

help the illiterate (though provision had been made, and was still made, for this by the minister reading through the whole portion of the psalm to be sung when he intimated it, as some oddly enough do still), and in Scotland lining persisted long after any need for it had passed. Its deplorable effect upon congregational singing surpasses the power of the mind to imagine.

During this period worship sank to a new low level, together with Church life in general. Cromwell, when he gained power and occupied Scotland, forbade the General Assembly to meet, as, to put it mildly, the Scottish ministers did not see eye to eye with him. Thus, for many years there was no coherent policy directed by its supreme court within the Church, and the rise of the two bellicose parties, Resolutioners and Protesters, divided the Church into two bitterly quarrelsome camps. The result, we need not be surprised to see, was that most ministers within their parishes went their own way without much let or hindrance; and many traditions cherished by the early Reformers fell into decay or desuetude, and we have now entered upon a sad and melancholy period when worship became tedious and dismal in the extreme, and continued so for a century or more.

Kirkton's fulsome description of the felicity of Church life during this period, written many years later, is utterly untrue, and at variance with all the records. Nicol, who was favourable to the Covenants, writes in 1651 what is more nearly true: 'Under heaven there was not greater falsehood, aggression, division, hatred, pride, malice, and envy, than was at this time, and divers and sundry years before, ever since the subscribing of the Covenant, every man seeking himself and his own rule, even under cloak of piety, which did cover much knavery.'[1]

[1] *Diary*, 59, 60. See also Kirkton's *History*, pp. 48-65.

V

Worship after the Restoration

CHARLES II, two years after he came to the throne of England, restored episcopacy in Scotland; but the bishops, seeking peace and ensuing it, gave a minimum of directions concerning worship, and except in the dioceses of the north and east they appear to have had little effect upon what was done. These directions most people would now agree were everywhere moderate and reasonable, genuinely designed to further the peace of the Church, and in no way exceeding old Scottish custom established at the Reformation and continuing through long years afterwards. Once again, had not tempers been inflamed, and sides irretrievably taken, they might well have succeeded. But history does not exist apart from persons, and the historian must try to see persons not ideally but as they are or were.

In the diocese of Aberdeen, the bishop enacted with the consent of his synod, only nine being absent, that there should be readers of the Scriptures in every parish, who were to use set forms of prayer, especially the Lord's Prayer, and were to read portions from the Psalter and Old Testament, to repeat the creed, to read from the New Testament, and to conclude by rehearsing the Ten Commandments. The minister's service, along familiar lines, was to follow. Private baptism and private communion were not to be denied when earnestly desired,

and the Directory was forbidden.[1] People were to stand
or kneel at prayer, 'these being the most reverent postures',
and they were to stand for the doxology. All this was
acceptable to the great majority of the clergy and people
in the diocese, who seem cordially to have complied.
Indeed, in the diocese of Aberdeen these injunctions represented little, if any, change.

The Synod of Edinburgh met under its bishop, and
was attended by fifty-eight ministers. The bishop preached
from Philippians 4.5, 'Let your moderation be known unto
all men', and the synod proceeded with its business. It
agreed to these modest proposals about worship: that
there should be daily prayer, morning and evening, in
all burgh churches, and in such others where numbers
could be collected; that the Lord's Prayer should be said
at least once at each service; that the doxology should
be used at the end of the metrical psalms, and that the
creed should be said at baptism.

Most ministers from Angus, Mearns, and Perthshire
attended the Synod of St. Andrews, but few from Fife.
The new primate enjoined his clergy to substitute the
reading of Holy Scripture for lecturing, to use the Lord's
Prayer and doxology at all services and the creed at
baptism.

The saintly Leighton, when at length he had been
persuaded to accept a bishopric, met his clergy at Dunblane, only a few being absent. They unanimously agreed
to these proposals of the bishop:

1. That instead of lecturing and preaching both at one
meeting, larger portions of the Holy Scriptures, one whole
chapter at least from each Testament, and Psalms withal, be
constantly read; and this, not as a byework while they are

[1] On the civil side (for use of the Directory had been enacted by Parliament as well as by the General Assembly), the Directory was rescinded
by the Act Rescissory, which annulled all statutes passed by Parliament
since 1640.

convening, but after the people are well-convened and the
worship solemnly begun with confession of sins and prayer,
either by the minister or some fit person by him appointed.

2. That the Lord's Prayer be restored to more frequent
use, and likewise the doxology and creed.

3. That daily public prayer in churches, morning and
evening, with reading the Scriptures, be used where it can
be had conveniently and the people exhorted to frequent
them, not so as to think that this should excuse them from
daily private prayer in their families and in secret, but rather
as a help to enable and dispose them more for both these.
And let the constant use of secret prayer be recommended to
all persons, as the great instrument of sanctifying the soul,
and of entertaining and increasing the love of God.

4. That the younger sorts and ignorant be diligently catechized at fit times all the year through, and so this be not
wholly laid over on some days or weeks before the celebration
of the Communion, but that the trial at that time be rather
of their good conversation [manner of life] and due disposition
for partaking that holy ordinance. . . .

5. That ministers use some short form of catechizing, such
as they may require account of, till some common form be
agreed on.

6. That preaching be plain and useful for all capacities,
not entangled with useless questions and disputes, nor continued to wearisome length; the great and most necessary
principles of religion most frequently treated upon, and often-
times larger portions of Scripture explained, and suitable
instructions and exhortations thence deduced.[1]

The prevalent system of preaching is described by
Burnet:

The preachers went all on one track, of raising observa-
tions on points of doctrine out of their text, and proving
these by reasons,[2] and then of applying those and proving

[1] Grub, *Ecclesiastical History of Scotland*, iii. pp. 201-5.
[2] The 'reasons' consisted largely of the quoting of texts from Holy
Scripture, very often without consideration of their context, and thus
anything could be 'proved'.

them by reasons, and showing the use that was to be made
on a point of doctrine, both for instruction and terror, for
exhortation and comfort, for trial of themselves upon it, and
for furnishing them with proper direction and helps; and this
was so methodical that the people grew to follow a sermon
through every branch of it.

This was the method adopted by the Directory. Baillie,
with far from approbation, describes a new type of sermon. He is speaking of Andrew Gray, a young minister
newly settled in Glasgow:

He has the new guise of preaching which Mr. Hew Binning
and Mr. Robert Leighton began, contemning [detesting] the
ordinary way of exponing and dividing a text, and of raising
doctrines and uses; but runs out in a discourse on some
common head, in a high, romancing, unscriptural style, tick-
ling the ear for the present, and moving the affections in
some, but leaving, as he confesses, little or nought to the
memory or understanding. This we must misken [ignore],
for we cannot help it.[1]

Baillie's account of the 'new preaching' is clearly somewhat overdrawn; and there is no doubt that the old
method was in need of some reform. Andrew Gray, at
any rate, won great popularity in Glasgow by the fresh-
ness and vividness of his preaching.

The Synod of Galloway met on 26 October 1664, and
made this enactment:

The which day it being represented to the Bishop and
Synod that notwithstanding of former acts made and standing in force for an uniformitie in practise among the bretheren
of the respective Presbyteries within this Diocesse, that is to
say that every minister should close his prayer, by saying of
the Lords prayer, should close the psalme with the doxologie,
should require of every parent at the baptizing of his child

[1] *Letters*, iii, p. 258.

the articles of his faith, should pray for his Majestie according to the titles that are in practise, as also for the Archbishops and Bishops, as also that there should be reading of the scriptures instead of lecturing in the publick congregations before the sermon in the forenoon. Yet they having heard that some of the bretheren within the Diocesse have not been carefull to put in practise these duties. Therefore the Bishop and Synod ordaines, likeas by this present act they require, every minister presently to put in practise these duties, and that the Moderators of every Presbytry inquire hereanent and see that the samen be duly done, and to be ready to give an account of their diligence as they will be answerable at the next Synod.[1]

No records of the other synods remain, but the marked similarity of the proposals preserved suggests that the bishops had previously reached agreement among themselves; and it is noticeable that all these proposals are merely what was customary in presbyterian times after the Reformation, before excessive English Puritan influences made themselves felt. So many people nowadays wax indignant about English influences in our worship, conveniently forgetting, if indeed they know, that most of what they defend as 'Scottish' is no more or less than English Puritanism from which all their notions derive, and that what they condemn is not 'Anglican' but part of our common inheritance from Christendom.

The synods were well attended in the north and east, but not in the south and west. No one attended, for example, in the dioceses of Argyll and Galloway except the deans, and at Glasgow only thirty-two ministers out of some 240 came to the synod. In the south and west the Protesters were the strong party; elsewhere the Resolutioners were much in the majority.

To examine into the tortuous questions and contentions that exercised the Church concerning the covenants,

[1] *Register of the Synod of Galloway, 1664-1671* (Kirkcudbright, 1856), p. 9. Act anent uniformity among Ministers.

episcopacy, the powers of the king, and other matters falls outside the scope of these studies, yet the question of worship cannot be treated *in vacuo*, for these controversies affected it at every point and certain aspects of worship were never at this time considered in the light of their own worth or merit but were made red-hot focal points of the contesting parties. The outed ministers at their conventicles, as also no doubt the great majority of those who took advantage of the various indulgences offered and returned to their parishes in the south and west, omitted in their services every proposal the bishops made; and whatever were the reasons they arrayed for so doing, the basic reason, not always consciously operative, was their ecclesiastical and political bias.

Thus, now and later, the reading of Holy Scripture in the churches, the singing of the doxology, the use of the Lord's Prayer and the creed came to be associated in people's minds with episcopacy, and consequently to be rejected by most who disliked bishops—in spite of the fact that all these things belonged to the Reformed Church in Knox's time.[1] As M'Crie has said,

It will be noted that the ritual modifications . . . recommended or enjoined by the Episcopal synods of the Restoration do not amount to very much; and, further, that supposing them all to be carried out, the effect would simply be to modify the ritual of the Westminster Directory in the way of falling back upon the Book of Common Order. There is not one of the details now mentioned which had not, at one time or another, found a place in the public worship of presbyterian Scotland, although English influence and Irish immigration may have resulted in some of them falling into disuse.[2]

[1] It is noticeable, however, that neither side abandoned preaching, although it was common to both. Had they done so, a chief means of carrying on their vitriolic controversies would have been lost. So it occurred to no presbyterian or episcopalian to refuse to preach merely because preaching was practised by the opposing party.

[2] M'Crie, op. cit., p. 231.

In the meantime, many of the bishops and clergy laboured quietly in their dioceses and parishes to retain this minimum. Leighton's synod of 1666 at Dunblane throws light upon a complex situation, if we trouble ourselves to reflect upon the forces at work behind these phrases:

The enactments of former synods as to the reading of Scripture, the recitation of the creed and the ten commandments during worship were renewed. The clergy were recommended to prefer long texts and short sermons to the short texts and very long discourses then common, which it was stated were apt to be more wearisome than profitable to the hearers. In any event, they were requested not to have their expositions on the same occasion with the sermons, as these, besides their tediousness, were apt to increase in the people's minds their foolish prejudice against hearing the Scriptures read without a discourse in addition; in which respect, notwithstanding their zeal against popery, they seemed to be too much of the Romish opinion that the Scriptures could not safely be allowed without a continual exposition to aid their obscurity. The ministers were enjoined to reduce the people from their unbecoming deportment during public worship, particularly their most indecent practice of sitting in time of prayer [this appears to have come in during Cromwell's time], and to persuade them either to kneel or stand, so that both with bodies and with souls, they might worship Him who was made both soul and body for that very end, in accordance with the invitatory now so much forgotten: 'O come, let us worship and bow down, and kneel before the Lord our maker.' Injunctions were also given to warn the people against neglect in attending at the celebration of the Holy Communion, as it was one of the chief defects of the Scottish Church that this great ordinance, so conducive to the increase of holiness, was seldom administered.[1]

In Glasgow, it is interesting to note in passing, a

[1] Leighton, *Works*, iv, pp. 398-401.

cathedral and university city, under six successive archbishops, and with parochial clergy, holy communion was
celebrated only twice during the twenty-eight years of
the second episcopacy, once under Leighton and once
under Burnet. Between 1645 and the Restoration, under
presbyterianism, there were six celebrations of holy communion—not frequent certainly, but it is a mere matter
of history that even in a period of disorganization celebrations under presbyterianism were more frequent than
they were under episcopacy during the second episcopate.[1]

But controversy and contention continued, intensified
and embittered by political divergencies; and our Scots
capacity for obduracy and no compromise, together with
our gift for pretty invective, displayed itself on a remarkable scale, even for us. Leighton eventually, after a short
period as acting-Archbishop at Glasgow (he was never
installed) gave up in 1673 the dismal struggle so uncon-
genial to his mind and nature, and retired to the south of
England, if possible to find peace and quiet. During this
brief time, however, he had quite won the hearts of the
Glasgow folk, and when it was recognized that he had
gone south to resign, a deputation waited on the magistrates 'entreating and desiring them' to try to prevent
his demission, declaring 'that the whoill citie and incor-
poratiouns therin hes lived peaceably and quietlie since
the said archbishop his coming to this burgh, throw his
christian cariage and behaviour towards them, and by his
government with great discretioune and moderatioune'.[2]
Nevertheless, men's minds were too disturbed, their feelings too acutely aroused, their prejudices too blatantly
marshalled, and their consciences too deeply committed,
to reach any settlement even of the most reasonable kind.

In the north only was it wholly otherwise, and Henry
Scougal's form of daily morning and evening prayer in

[1] Leishman, op. cit., v, pp. 394, 390.   [2] Burgh Records, 2 May 1673.

I

St. Machar's Cathedral, Aberdeen,[1] illustrates the moderation and sobriety that prevailed there. Henry Scougal, the son of Bishop Patrick Scougal, was professor of divinity at King's College. 'The first impression' these prayers make on us, writes Dr. Wilson Baird, 'is their likeness to the "good" extempore prayer to which our fathers were accustomed. They abound in expressions familiar in the "floating liturgy" of the Church of Scotland. They are reverent, sonorous, dignified. . . . One is tempted to dally with the possibilities which this type of prayer held out for the orderly development of public worship on national lines. Even if it be admitted that here we do not find either the beauty or succinctness of the language of the Book of Common Prayer, we can imagine easily enough how on these lines Scottish worship might have grown in richness and in adequacy and at the same time retained the allegiance of the common folk of Scotland.' These prayers are in style not unlike the prayers we find proposed earlier in the 1616 and 1619 books, or indeed some of those later proposed in England in the numerous suggested alternatives to the Book of Common Prayer from the Savoy Liturgy on through the eighteenth and early nineteenth centuries.[2]

The greatest extreme, on the other hand, is probably represented in the sect founded by John Gib, a shipmaster at Bo'ness, described in the language of the day as 'a great professor'. Those who followed him deserted their families and work alike, and went out into the fields, hearing their preachers and testifying 'against the wickedness of the times'. In 1681 their leaders, arrested and imprisoned,

[1] Edited by Dr. J. Wilson Baird, in *Church Service Society Annual*, 1936-7, pp. 47-56; also reprinted, inter alia, in Hall, *Fragmenta Liturgica*, ii. pp. 95-109.

[2] Cf. many of the prayer-books mentioned in my *Book of Common Prayer and the Worship of the Non-Anglican Churches*; see also A. Elliott Peaston, *The Prayer Book Reform Movement in the XVIIIth Century*.

sent a paper to the Privy Council. They declared that they had cut out the metrical psalms from their Bibles and burned them as being no part of the Scriptures; that they renounced chapters and verses on the same ground, and indeed condemned the translations of both Testaments, the Long and Shorter Catechisms, the Confession of Faith, the Acts of the General Assembly, and the covenants, and renounced the names of months and days, except the Sabbath.[1] Little seemed left.

There were broadly three groups of presbyterian ministers at this time: those who were presbyterian by preference, but were not so strongly committed in mind and conscience that they could not accept episcopacy, and these remained undisturbed in their parishes; those whose views were much stronger, but who eventually accepted one of the indulgences and were re-admitted to their parishes; those who would not accept any indulgence, and remained outside the Church. After 1681 these last were organized as the United Societies, and it was from them that most of the martyrs came.

The worship of the outed ministers was not greatly different from that of many of the others, and it conformed to the general pattern that we have described. It must have been almost precisely similar to the worship conducted by the indulged ministers in their parishes. Here is a description, for example, of a celebration of holy communion from the pen of John Blackadder,[2] a famous covenanter in the south-east of Scotland, who conducted his last conventicle before arrest on the hill behind the church in my own parish.

The service he describes took place in 1677 at East Nisbet, Berwickshire. It began with 'prefacing'; this practice had come in about the second decade of the seventeenth century as a fairly brief exhortation and summons

[1] Grub, op. cit., iii, p. 263.   [2] In his *Memoirs*, pp. 200-1.

to prayer before the minister's service began,[1] and as time passed these items became a good deal longer. In the Westminster Assembly there was discussion about whether this practice should be recommended in the Directory, although it was generally customary in both kingdoms; and the opening exhortation 'Dearly beloved' &c.[2] at matins and evensong in the Book of Common Prayer affords a further example of this attachment to 'prefacing'. It was finally allowed, and at this period was practised in Scotland by presbyterians and episcopalians alike.

The prefacing was followed by a psalm, prayers, the sermon, and the intercessions.

The place where we convened [writes Blackadder] was in every way commodious, and seemed to have been formed on purpose. It was a green and pleasant haugh, fast by the water-side [the Whitadder]. In both directions there was a spacious brae, in form of a half-round, covered with delightful pasture, and rising with a gentle slope to a goodly height. Above us was the clear blue sky, for it was a sweet and calm Sabbath morning. . . . The Communion Tables[3] were spread on the green by the water; and around them the people had arranged themselves in decent order. But far the greater multitude sat on the brae-face, which was crowded from top to bottom. The Tables were served by some gentlemen, persons of the gravest deportment. None were admitted without tokens as usual, which were distributed on the Saturday, but only to such as were known to the ministers. . . . All the regular forms were gone through; the communicants entered at one end, and retired at the other, the way being kept clear for them to take their seats again on the hillside. Mr. Welsh

[1] Examples are numerous in Alexander Henderson's *Sermons, Prayers, and Pulpit Addresses*, published Edinburgh, 1867.

[2] This was first prefaced to Matins (Morning Prayer) in 1552, but was duplicated and prefaced also to Evening Prayer in 1662.

[3] In addition to the two long tables at which the communicants sat along one side, there was 'one short one across the head, with seats at each side', at which the officiating ministers sat. The tables, thus arranged, formed a U.

preached the action sermon, and served the first two Tables; the other four ministers, Mr. Blackadder, Mr. Dickson, Mr. Riddel, and Mr. Rae, exhorted the rest in turn. The Table services were closed by Mr. Welsh, with solemn thanksgiving. The Communion was peaceably concluded,[1] all the people heartily offering up their gratitude, and singing with a joyful noise to the Rock of their salvation.[2] It was pleasant as night fell[3] to hear their melody swelling in full unison along the hills. . . . About 100 sat at every Table; there were 16 Tables served, so that about 3,200 communicated that day. The afternoon sermon was preached by Mr. Dickson, and the season of solemn services was brought to a close with a sermon on Monday afternoon by Mr. Blackadder.

During the second episcopacy, the General Assembly or General Synod, as it would have been called, did not meet, although many of the bishops desired one to be convened. Archbishop Sharp, a former presbyterian, always resolutely opposed the proposal. Thus, while the bishops met their synods, no court representative of the whole Church met during this period.

As time passed, there were those both of episcopalian and presbyterian preference who would have wished to see a liturgy used; but nothing ever came of this. It was felt by the civil authorities and the primate alike (he had no wish 'to ride the ford' where his predecessor drowned[4])

[1] Warnings had gone out that Lord Home and a body of horse were out to put down the conventicle, and many of those attending had come armed. But no clash occurred.

[2] Metrical Psalm 95.

[3] The service began in the morning, fairly early, and lasted with the afternoon sermon until nightfall; this became generally common in the early part of the next century.

[4] Row, *Life of Robert Blair*, p. 563. In his wonderfully faithful and just description of these difficult times in *Old Mortality*, Sir Walter Scott errs radically in attributing to young Morton of Milnwood fidelity in saying the responses at the services in his parish church where the incumbent was an indulged minister. Responses were used by no party in the Scottish Church at this time, and the Book of Common Prayer in no parish church. Probably prayers from the prayer-book were often used, not read but committed to memory.

that this would stir up furious trouble, in view of the past.
Thus worship was not seriously interfered with at any
point—and there was no attempt made even to persuade
communicants to kneel to receive communion, but the
old custom remained everywhere of sitting at the Lord's
table. The most that ever occurred was an enactment of
the Privy Council in 1680, formally sanctioning the Book
of Common Prayer for family worship, and numbers of
the Book of Common Prayer were sold at this time in
Scotland, while evidence exists also that copies of the
Scottish prayer-book (1637) were in private possession
and show signs of much handling.

Illustrative of worship during this period, we may quote
the description of Thomas Morer, an English Army chap-
lain, stationed in Scotland in 1690.[1]

The Episcopalian Church have hitherto used no liturgy at
all, no more than the Presbyterians who now govern, and
their whole service on the Lord's day . . . depends on these
particulars: First, the precentor, about half an hour before
the preacher comes, reads two or three chapters to the congregation of what part of Scripture he pleases or as the
minister gives him directions. As soon as the preacher gets
into the pulpit, the precentor leaves reading, and sets a psalm,
singing with the people till the minister, by some sign, orders
him to give over.[2] The psalm over, the preacher begins,
confessing sins and begging pardon, exalting the holiness and
majesty of God, and setting before Him our vileness and propensity to transgress His commandments. Then he goes to
sermon, delivered by heart, and therefore sometimes spoiled
by battologies, little impertinences, and incoherence in their

---

[1] *Ecclesiastical Records*, Spalding Club, lxix; Morer's *Short Account of
Scotland* was printed in London in 1702. Boswell described Morer as 'a
man of various enquiry', and lent the book to Johnson. 'JOHNSON. "It
is sad stuff, Sir, miserably written, as books in general then were. There
is now an elegance of style universally diffused." '

[2] As the Pope did at the introit in the early Roman services (see p. 4
supra).

discourses.[1] The sermon finished, he returns to prayer; thanks God for the opportunities to deliver His word; prays for all mankind, for all christians, for that particular nation, for the sovereign and royal family without naming any, for subordinate magistrates, for sick people, especially such whose names the precentor hands up to him,[2] then concludes with the Lord's Prayer, to sanctify what was said before.[3] After this, another psalm is sung, named by the minister, and frequently suited to the subject of his sermon; which done, he gives the benediction, and dismisses the congregation for that time. The afternoon service follows soon after, 'because in the interim they eat nothing', and is a repetition of the first service.

The difference between the Episcopalians and Presbyterians can scarcely be discerned in their worship, he says: 'and therefore we the more admire [wonder] that the two parties should so much disagree between themselves when they appear to the world so like brethren. . . . Truly their difference is hardly discernible; for their singing of psalms, praying, preaching, and collection are the same, and 'tis the whole of their worship in both congregations. They both do it after the same manner, saving that after the psalm the Episcopalian minister uses the doxology, which the other omits, and concludes his own prayer with that of the Lord, which the Presbyterian refuses to do.'

The Lord's Supper, he says, is rarely celebrated, perhaps

[1] Most published sermons of the period suggest that this is an understatement.

[2] A charmingly unaffected restoration of an early Christian practice of praying for persons by name which appears to have been long customary. In the Tyninghame records, for example, we have this note of April 1637: 'This day threttie-and-three pepile prayed for in the Kirk'; and in April 1648 mention is made of a woman 'quha was beddral [bed-ridden] these ffour yeirs bygaine and blind, being always publicklie prayed for'. It is possible that it was a pre-Reformation practice in Scotland, as elsewhere, but evidence is lacking.

[3] The use of the Lord's Prayer suggests that Morer is probably describing a service conducted by an episcopalian minister; it is the only mark of difference between the parties in this description.

once or twice a year, the congregation sitting; and burials take place without a minister.

The Scottish bishops, all firm Jacobites and incapable of the compromise effected by most of the Anglican episcopate, went out on purely political grounds with the Stuart King in 1689, and presbyterianism was reestablished.[1] This description dates from the time when the changeover from episcopacy[2] had just been made, but no changes had yet been effected in the worship of either party.

However, as the Protesters were now become the dominant party in the Church, and controlled the General Assembly and the presbyteries, worship was soon reduced to its extreme bare limits. Grey Graham perhaps paints the picture somewhat severely, but it is broadly true to say with him that 'of the Presbyterian clergy who had been ejected from their parishes in 1662 when episcopacy was established, there were about sixty surviving. These old men were now restored to their charges, and in the first General Assembly which met in 1690 they were the leaders and oracles, although there were associated with them seventy-six ministers who had been "indulged" to preach in 1687, and forty-three elders. To those men were given by Parliament powers which they were not fit to wield with fairness and tenderness.'[3] Yet, when we consider what they had faced for conscience' sake, and the hardships they had undergone, we may feel that they exercised greater restraint and charity than was common

[1] The Westminster Confession of Faith but not the Directory is mentioned in the Act (1 Parl. of William and Mary, 2 sess., 7 June 1690).

[2] On the worship of the episcopalians who remained outside the Church of Scotland, see W. Perry, *The Scottish Prayer Book*, and his *The Oxford Movement in Scotland*, J. Dowden, *The Scottish Communion Office*, and P. A. Lemprière, *Scottish Communion Offices of 1637, 1735, 1755, 1764, 1889*.

[3] Grey Graham, *The Social Life of Scotland in the Eighteenth Century*, p. 269. The more extreme of the 'outed' presbyterian ministers refused to re-enter the Church, adhering invincibly to the covenants, and many had been executed or driven into exile during the last persecutions.

in that age.[1] The position described by Grey Graham
was quickly changed by subsequent Acts of Parliament.
An Act of 1693 allowed episcopalian ministers to retain
their charges on taking the oath of allegiance and submitting to presbyterian government, and an Act of 1695
allowed episcopalians to remain on taking the oath of
allegiance but without participating in the presbyterian
organization or courts. Thus, large numbers remained
within the Church. To estimate the number of permanently 'outed' episcopalians is difficult, and accuracy
impossible. There were those 'rabbled' in 1688-9, estimated variously from 100-200; those deprived in 1689
for refusing to pray for William and Mary, estimated at
180. To both these dispossessed groups the Acts of 1693
and 1695 held out nothing, for the Acts applied only to
those who had remained in possession. The episcopalians
remaining within the Church of Scotland included both
those who conformed to presbytery and those who were
'indulged', but also included especially in the north a
considerable number who neither conformed nor were
indulged but who could not be displaced. It is said
generally that 165 episcopalians were in their parishes in
1707, by which time many of the 1690 men would be
dead, and this number probably does not include men
who conformed to presbytery. The number outside at
this time might have been some 200-300, certainly not
more, perhaps less, and many of these may have gone
to England to be settled in parishes there.

[1] They could of course show resolution too. John Dysart, a graduate of
Glasgow who had served in England during the troubles, was inducted at
Coldingham in 1694. 'On the occasion of his settlement, a military force
had to be present to prevent a riot, most of the parishioners being attached
to episcopacy. Thereafter, for some time, he was accustomed to carry
pistols with him to the pulpit, which he laid down openly, on each side
of him.' He became moderator of the Synod of Merse and Teviotdale in
1701, and lived to the good age of 72, dying in 1732 (*Diary of the Rev. Geo.
Turnbull, Minister of Alloa and Tyninghame, 1657-1704*, Scot. Hist. Soc.,
pp. 405-6).

In the worship of the establishment, except among some of the old Resolutioners and indulged episcopalians, the Lord's Prayer, doxology, creed, and reading of Holy Scripture were not used. 'Lecturing', however, was encouraged by an Act passed in 1694: 'considering how necessary and edifying it is that the people be well acquainted with the Holy Scriptures', the Assembly 'doth therefore recommend . . . that the ministers . . . in the exercise of lecturing, read and open up to the people some large and considerable portion of the Word of God; and this to the effect the old custom introduced and established by the Directory may by degrees be recovered'.[1] This recommendation makes it clear that 'a considerable portion' of the Holy Scriptures was to be read; but man's words gained the ascendancy, and although the expositions were 'large and considerable' the amount of Scripture read in the process was small. The framers of the Directory themselves tried to prevent this abuse by recommending 'that if it is deemed necessary or desirable to furnish elucidation or explanation, this ought not to be interjected in the reading, but be reserved till the close'; but the injunction was universally ignored. This insistence upon lecturing was in part, of course, a hit at the episcopalians who had no taste for it; and it will be remembered that this dislike of lecturing (evident in the Directory itself) was shared by most Scottish ministers before 1640.

More and more these matters became party badges vauntingly worn, their use governed by no considerations of worship, doctrine, or common sense; and the controversy sharpened when Queen Anne ascended the throne, for it was then expected that an Act would be passed to benefit the episcopalians.

Pamphlets innumerable by those who feared and those who

[1] *Acts of Assembly*, p. 239.

hoped for it were published, making the most of points in which they differed, among others those of worship. This controversy throws much light on the new state of things. The Directory was a sharp weapon in the hands of the Episcopalian combatants when they had to speak of such things as lessons of Scripture and the Lord's prayer. No doubt these taunts promoted the passing of an Act of Assembly in 1705, which recommended for the first time since the Revolution a better observance of the Directory.[1]

The Act referred to is that of Session 10: 'The General Assembly seriously recommends to all ministers and others within this National Church the due observance of the Directory for the Public Worship of God, approved by the General Assembly held in the year 1645, Sess. 10.' Another Act directed against episcopalian 'innovations' in worship was passed in 1707, arising out of the active attempt to circulate by charity from England free copies of the Book of Common Prayer. It was a long Act, but the meat of it was in the restatement of an old principle: 'nothing is to be admitted to the worship of God, but what is prescribed in the Holy Scriptures'—a principle, often still proclaimed, not so simple of either interpretation or practice as at first glance it appears to be.

Psalmody became, if possible, even more dismal, made so by the total disappearance of part-singing and the continuance of the insufferable practice of 'lining out'; and there was no musical recovery until more than half a century had passed. People sat to sing, led by the precentor, who was usually the schoolmaster.

The attitude at prayer grew slovenly and careless, sitting being common, and kneeling all too uncommon in spite of its having been universal in Reformed and old Scottish practice. Gradually, however, standing at prayer—once practised only among episcopalians—became general, and

[1] Leishman, op. cit., v, p. 399.

presently was thought to be a good old distinctively presbyterian custom. Pamphlets of the period mention kneeling, sitting, and standing, and all were to be seen even within the one congregation, but sitting was more generally favoured. Episcopalians at first made a point of always standing, but there was,

especially among those who qualified for Government, a growing feeling in favour of kneeling. In time, church people seem to have given up their unseemly attitude of sitting, but they did not return to their own earlier custom. Standing became general, and, with other observances of no very remote origin is earnestly defended at the present time by many who look back on the expanse of their church history with a scope of vision too limited to take in foreground and distance, but able only to rest on the space between.[1]

Men sat in church, except during prayer, with their heads covered; and ministers often still wore their caps, as they had done in times past, while preaching. It had long been common everywhere in church during sermon for men to remain covered, and was only beginning to be given up in England by 1703, while it persisted in many parts of Scotland for more than half a century longer. In the Netherlands, the minister still carries his cap into the pulpit, although he no longer wears it but hangs it on a peg provided for it beneath the tester.

Ministers on the whole abandoned robes, and did not resume them until towards the end of the century, and wore them then only in the churches. Till the second episcopacy robes had been universally worn since (and before) the Reformation, and even in the 1650s Patrick Gillespie had preached before Cromwell 'in his velvet rarely-cut cassock'. But after the Restoration, robes began to be regarded as a mark of episcopacy, and the black gown became the hated badge of 'black prelacy'; and in

[1] Leishman, op. cit., v, p. 401.

1688-9 when many episcopalians were expelled from their parishes, it became an exciting pastime of the mob to drag the 'curates' from their manses, stripping them of their robes. These robes were not surplices, which were never worn in Scotland, but cassocks and 'Genevan' gowns. Thus, black being associated with episcopacy, blue became a favourite colour for ministers' cloaks and clothes, and the phrase 'true-blue presbyterians' may have referred to clothes as well as banners. For headgear they wore a three-cornered hat.

Visiting Scotland in 1709, Calamy says, 'The ministers, even in the most solemn auditories, preached with neck-cloths and coloured cloaks, which a little surprised me. It was their common way, unless they were professors of divinity, or persons remarkable for age or gravity.'[1] Calamy, who at this time was the presbyterian minister at Westminster and a lecturer at Salter's Hall, was a leading English Puritan who had not only lived in England but had studied and travelled abroad; and his learning was so highly esteemed in Scotland that during his visit he was laureated by the universities of Glasgow, Aberdeen, and Edinburgh. But with all his Puritan views, he was surprised to find robes so seldom worn in Scotland.

In addition to the complexity of episcopalian and presbyterian opinions, and the constant war between the two, after the Union of 1707, 'dislike of everything English was keen in the north; a contempt of everything Scottish was bitter in the south. Communication with England was rare even among people of quality: for distances were great, roads were execrable, and the cost of travelling and lodging was appalling to people who, in all ranks, high and low, were miserably poor.'[2] This added to the strong and unreasoning dislike among presbyterians of anything that was thought to be Anglican or episcopalian usage.

[1] See also Leishman, op. cit., pp. 402-3. [2] Grey Graham, op. cit., pp. 1, 2.

Nor did the savage famines of the 1690s make men less bitter: the hardness of life nurtured hard, stern minds.

Yet there was some accommodation,[1] and all was not unreserved contention. Even in collegiate churches colleagues were sometimes of opposite parties, yet managed to live in some peace together, as in Dunfermline and Haddington where till 1724 one minister had his forenoon service with the Lord's Prayer, doxology, and Apostles' Creed; and in the afternoon the other omitted 'these obnoxious prelatic superfluities'. They were, of course, often called harder names, if we care to burrow about for them in the pamphlets of the period; but to do so arouses only disgust that earnest and serious but too obviously fanatical men could so far forget themselves as to apply such epithets to things so sacred as the Lord's Prayer. In 1698 we have the kirk-session of St. Mary's, Whitekirk, resolving to use the Lord's Prayer, Ten Commandments, and Creed at the Sunday services, and the then incumbent was of presbyterian sympathies.[2] In the north, many of the practices common since the Reformation continued to prevail.[3]

Apart from the few differences mentioned the rest of the worship was largely indistinguishable between the parties. For commanding common assent were general similarities in the whole structure and method of worship. Both parties used extempory prayer, and both had much the same rough vocabulary; both used the metrical psalms, rejected organs, and favoured 'lining'. Only a

[1] See p. 138 infra, on Lord's Prayer.

[2] 27 November 1698, the Session 'appoint the precentor too read every lords day the beliefe and the lords prayer and the ten commands, aye untill such time as the schoolars repeat the catechisms [in which these were included] in the church', for repetition of these by the people had ceased (Turnbull, *Diary*).

[3] In 1690 there was only one presbyterian minister in the Synod of Aberdeen and Banff, in which there were 100 parishes; in 1697, only fifteen presbyterian ministers (Spalding *Miscellany*, ii, p. 72).

few kept the Christian festivals, except occasionally Christmas,[1] and more rarely Easter and Whitsun. All took communion sitting at forms at the long table; all used tokens; and all rigidly fenced the tables. And the statements that Holy Scripture was not read at all in the services are often, but certainly not always, exaggerated— one group read them *simpliciter*, and the other group interspersed an exposition. There were many, however, who read very little indeed—a few verses—and probably none read the chapter from each Testament recommended by the Directory. Both were rigorous in discipline and austere unbending sabbatarians. Private baptism was practised by both; both omitted funeral services; and both were given to long extemporary sermons. Compared with the similarities, the differences between presbyterians and episcopalians were indeed superficial.

The character of the ministers of both parties has been exposed to praise or blame by the contending pamphleteers. 'In the incessant war of pamphlets which was maintained for a generation', writes Grey Graham without any exaggeration, 'there is a spirit of intense virulence. So charged with venom, so abounding in evident misrepresentation are the accusations of Presbyterian and Episcopalian alike, that it is well-nigh impossible to clear the way to truth amidst the jungle of reproaches, recriminations, charges and counter-charges.'[2] Yet it must be confessed as probable that examples could be found of all the charges made,[3] even if it be allowed that the pamphleteers selected the most scandalous episodes possible against each other, as no doubt they did; but there was a good deal of fire beneath the smoke.

Modern readers of many of these pamphlets must also

[1] Grey Graham, op. cit., p. 279, see footnote 5.

[2] ibid., pp. 274-8.   [3] See Burt's remark, p. 140 infra.

be struck by the unrestrained prurience and vulgarity of the writers of both parties, too gross and coarse to reprint but apart from which the age cannot be really understood, for this method of controversy even in religious matters shocked but few in an age which was far from delicate in referring to sex. Grey Graham and Lord Macaulay suggest that these pamphleteers were 'habitual liars'; but while they were extravagantly bigoted men who wallowed in gross exaggeration and were possessed of a strong taste for salacity, their pictures and portraits were not bereft of a basis of truth. But it is clear that moderation, sense, and charity were not conspicuous among these contenders: some were learned, and many ignorant, but all were imbued with fanaticism. And though most were earnest and honest men, they were 'apt to mistake fanaticism for earnestness', and to 'confound their antipathies with their duties'. It was not an atmosphere in which worship would flower into loveliness.

Nevertheless, there were many moderate men, like Sir Hugh Campbell of Calder, who strove to engender reason in the practices of the time. Sir Hugh had been a generous friend to outed ministers during the episcopacy, but he was irrevocably convinced that the Lord's Prayer should be used in the public services of the Church. And accordingly he fought a long battle through the press and the courts of the Church to achieve its restoration, and carried on an extensive private correspondence with various persons, among others Principal Carstares, appealing to Holy Scripture, ancient and universal custom, Scottish usage, and the Directory, but could get no direct official action.[1] An example of the type of person

---

[1] Carstares said that the Act of 1705 had been passed largely to appease Sir Hugh; this is no doubt true, but even when so pressed the Assembly would not specifically recommend the restoration of the Lord's Prayer, preferring to conceal the recommendation under a general exhortation to follow the Directory more closely.

he had to deal with is found in Hog of Carnock, who in 1705 wrote an essay[1] on the Lord's Prayer as a basis for instruction and devotion, but protested senselessly against its use in public worship: 'Seeing our antagonists make use of this as the special reason for concluding public prayer with these words . . . I must say it, and doubt not the concurrence of those who are exercised to godliness, that it is (in this sense) an engine of hell, not only far contrary to the divine prescript, but likewise perversive to the Gospel of Christ.' All those, however, who had been opposed to prelacy were not of this mind; Sir Hugh had a list of those ministers who used the Prayer, and it is certainly incomplete.

John Anderson of Dumbarton, though 'one of the most vigorous disputants against prelacy', also fought hard and successfully in his parish to restore the Lord's Prayer; and he has left us an instructive and entertaining narrative of the battle, or indeed campaign,[2] which followed hard upon the 1705 Act of the General Assembly. Anderson was minister at Dumbarton 1698-1718, and later at Ramshorn, Glasgow, where he created excitement by consecrating his new church. Of the Lord's Prayer, he says that his neighbour Wallace of Cardross 'had used it a twelvemonth before', and 'there was no noise made', though Cardross was considered to be more 'strict' than Dumbarton. Anderson, of course, was trying to introduce it to be said by himself; he intended nothing so advanced as its being said by all together! Mr. J. G. Coats writes: 'In 1711 Anderson conceived the idea of publishing in pamphlet form, anonymously, an imaginary

[1] Later, a well-known 'Marrow man', he wrote a *Casuistical Essay on the Lord's Prayer*.

[2] *Disquisition on the Introduction of the Lord's Prayer into Dumbarton*, 1705. I quote from a copy made from the original MS. in the hands of Anderson's descendant, Mrs. J. G. Coats, Glasgow. It has also been edited by Professor Cooper and printed in the Scottish Ecclesiological Society's *Transactions*, 1905.

K

"Dialogue between a Countryman and a Curat", strongly attacking the episcopalian liturgy. The challenge was taken up by a Scots episcopalian curate, Robert Calder, and a series of pamphlets resulted. These survive [among the family papers] with the exception of the last by Calder, which must have been very abusive to have evoked such a violent and undignified reply as Anderson's "Curat Calder Whipt". In these pamphlets, Anderson's arguments are able: some are provocative, some are sarcastic, and some are, I think, rather unfairly stated.' Wodrow writes of him, that he was 'a kind, frank, comradly man, *when not grated*'.[1]

Anderson's chronicle begins, 'Upon the 29 of Aprill 1705, which was the first Sabbath after my return to Dumbarton from the generall assembly,[2] I began to introduce the usage of the Lord's prayer in the public worship, annexing it to the prayer after sermon with this transition —all of which we beg through our Lord Jesus Christ, in whose words we pray as he hath commanded us, our father, etc.' After the closing psalm which followed, and before the benediction, he informed the congregation that the recent General Assembly had 'recommended the observation of the publick Directory for Worship to all ministers within this nationall Church', and pointed out that in it were directions for the use of the Lord's Prayer 'in the publick prayers of the Church', and then piously hoped that 'none of you will stumble at it'. But, 'the following week', he continues, 'I was informed, that notwithstanding this caution taken, there were severalle stumbled'. And indeed there were; and they stumbled through argument and explanation, through parish and presbytery, for several months. At times, things would seem to settle down peaceably, then something or other would stir the waters once more.

[1] *Analecta*, ii, p. 343.   [2] See p. 134, n. 1, supra.

Visits to Glasgow by his parishioners were not helpful. 'That which of all others was the greatest cause of the noise', we read, 'was that some of the people here, having gone occasionally to Glasgow, returning reported that the place was mightily alarmed with it, and this amused [bemused] people's minds here, and filled their mouths with objections, because Glasgow above all other people in the nation had the report of being best affected to presbytery, but surely their knowledge of its principles is but very indifferent'. Again he succeeded in 'solving scruples' and 'generally satisfying' his parishioners, when alas 'some of the people' went to the Glasgow communion and 'returned in the greatest fume imaginable, proclaiming that they had it from the ministers of Glasgow that there was no such thing done at the assembly as the recommending of the Directory'. For a month or more he was 'under the repute of a liar, and that in the pulpit', and his 'reputation had lyen bleeding most pitifully' until he obtained the printed Acts of Assembly and was able to vindicate himself. So it went on. We cannot trace the history in full detail but there is one episode Anderson records which it would seem a pity to miss.

About this time [he writes] there was a very pleasant incident fell out which I cannot but relate for discovering the weakness of country people's minds, and because it shows how apt they are to be amused even almost to a phrenzie on points of religion. There is a fenny marshy piece of ground, very full of reeds, called Rossriven, about half a mile up the Levin river from the town, on the other side: in the midst of all these heats, there comes thither a fowl called bittern, and by the country people, a blutter. There had been none of that kind in the country for a considerable time before. This fowl has a very hideous uncouth sound which we may express by bounging or blouting, as when one puts one's finger into an empty bottle and draws it out again hastily and with force.

And Dr. Brown, in his 'Vulgar Errors', gives an account of how it makes this sound, viz. by putting in and pulling out its beak out of a hollow reed. Those that first heard the fowl make this noise were mightily alarmed at it, and many of them affirmed it made the ground shake under them, and the hair stand on their heads; whereupon they concluded it to be no less than the devill. At length the report spread itself, and presently they applied it to the introduction of the Lord's prayer, and doubted not but some mighty evill was portended thereby. At last James Houston, a gunsmith in the town, who was acquaint with that kind of fowl and its sound, carries out his fowling piece and shoots it dead, after which the uncouth sound was never heard, and the people without much ado were undeceived. The Lord's day following, there was none observed to separate from the worship but one.

The controversy had lasted from May to October, but it died down when the Synod refused to adjudicate save to recommend uniformity among parishes, which, says Anderson, 'vexed them extremely when I told 'em the meaning of that recommendation was that they should use the Lord's prayer as I did'. 'On the Sunday after', he adds, 'I used it both before and after noon, which exposed the weak zealous brethren to much contempt, when the people saw how much they had been abused by them; and thenceforth I used it as my discretion suggested, without any scruple made by anybody.'

To Anderson's narrative we may attach the quaintly sweet story of old Mr. Patrick Simson, parish minister at Renfrew, a former covenanter and outed minister, which Wodrow[1] refers to as occurring a few years later, in 1710. The old gentleman had fallen into an extraordinary innovation, contrary to all his former custom; at his June communion 'after the Tables were over', says Wodrow, he 'fell a-discoursing, and gave some directions; and,

[1] *Analecta*, i., p. 287.

advising them to be much in prayer, commended the
Lord's Prayer, and concluded, they say, with it.' Simson
himself had a somewhat different version, and Wodrow
also records it as he received it from him: 'After the
Tables, he took occasion to observe that there were three
things that had Christ's name particularly given them:
the Lord's Day, and the Lord's Supper, and the Lord's
Prayer. After he had spoken awhile on the former two,
he spoke a little upon the use of the Lord's Prayer, and
first repeated it, and then prayed over the different petitions, with pretty large enlargements[1] upon each of them.'
He vindicated himself thus: 'For severall dayes before his
Communion he had a strong impression on his spirit, once
before he died to testify his communion with the whole
Christian Church, by the publick using of the Lord's
Prayer: That he was now 82 years [old], and many of
the young Ministers might have it to say that they never
heard this prayer made use of by the old men, and
make this a further excuse for the total disuse of it;
which he thought was a fault, though he was against the
abuse of it.'

We may now describe worship as it was, say about
1730, and shall not notice much change.

The services began usually shortly after the first bell,
rung from the tower or gable belfry, and more rarely from
a tree in the kirkyard. At the second bell, about 9 or
10 a.m., the people went into the church, and the precentor led the singing of a psalm, dolefully lining it out

[1] To enlarge upon the Lord's Prayer by praying upon each petition
was a practice at Strasbourg under Bucer in 1539; Calvin took it over into
his use in 1542. It was translated into English by Huycke in 1550, and
into Latin by Pullain in 1554 for use in the edition of his *Liturgia sacra* of
that year. It appeared first in the Book of Common Order in the 1565
edition, and is largely taken verbally from Huycke. No doubt old Mr.
Simson as a youth in the 1640s, when he was in his 'teens, had heard
such a paraphrase of the Lord's Prayer used, and he was now reverting
to it with the fondness of the old for days that are gone.

to a modal melody, and at the third bell the minister entered the pulpit, often hat on head, and bowed to the lairds who stood up to acknowledge his salutation. He signalled the precentor to conclude, and began the service with a long prayer, invariably at this time extemporary, delivered in a piously whining tone which had come down from the old 'antediluvians' and was still highly regarded. The efficacy of prayer was measured by its ardour and fluency, and not least by its fervid lengthiness. Those ministers who were great 'wrestlers' were most revered, and during their supplication they did indeed wrestle like Jacob with the angel till the 'sweet haled down' while the minister wept and smiled.[1]

After the first prayer, the lecture followed, occupying the large part of an hour, in which Scripture was explained verse by verse; then another prayer, somewhat briefer, followed by the sermon, delivered extemporary or by heart and about one hour in length; and afterwards a long prayer of thanksgiving and intercession, the concluding psalm, and the benediction. In the afternoon— the interval was short, for there was no hot meal on Sundays till the evening—the same order was repeated, with the lecture omitted.

[1] Many stories were and are told of the gauche, grotesque, intimate, and often coarse and banal utterances made during these prayers (and sermons). Burt (*Letters from the North*, i, 175) says of them: 'I have heard so many and of so many that I really think there is nothing in *Scots Presbyterian Eloquence* but has what at least is probable; nor were these things confined at this time to one party, for episcopalian ways and manners in *Episcopalian Eloquence display'd* leaves little choice between the two.' These two monstrous but popular pamphlets were often later bound together and enjoyed a large circulation, probably not so much because of their arguments as their anecdotes, most of which must have supplied good tavern gossip, if indeed they did not originate there. The authors, with remarkable reticence, issued their volumes anonymously, but *Presbyterian Eloquence* came from the vitriolic pen of the episcopalian, Robert Calder, and *Episcopalian Eloquence* was the presbyterian, George Ridpath's, no less vituperous and more extensively salacious reply. They are interesting, if not convincing, examples of the controversies and manners of the time.

Our picture of this period would be incomplete if we did not also include a description of the communion services as they developed in the eighteenth century. They were indeed awesome festivals. Known as 'the Action', 'the Great Work', 'the Sacred Solemnity', 'the Occasion', and 'the Sacrament', they involved, as old family documents abundantly bear witness, intense personal rededication.

During the first half of the century, generally speaking, holy communion was celebrated not more than once a year in each parish and sometimes much less frequently; but as many as eight or nine parishes would often combine for the event, closing their churches, so that, in spite of infrequent celebrations in their own parish, most people had in fact frequent opportunities for receiving communion. We have noted already how people came up from Dumbarton to Glasgow for the communion, and in the country they frequently travelled as far as forty to fifty miles to attend, walking or riding over the moors and tracks—there were no wheeled vehicles usable—from all directions.

The season chosen for communion services was usually from May to October, and before the day approached, ministers and elders were busy visiting and catechizing all families in their parishes, examining into doctrine and life, mending quarrels and reconciling disputants, and within the kirk-session itself submitting one another to a rigorous scrutiny. There were other matters too which demanded much preparation: when sometimes there were ten to twelve thousand communicants and even in remote parishes as many as one thousand, the problems of catering and hospitality were formidable in days when food was scarce and shelter strictly limited, as during the first half of the century. Nor are we to forget that it was a point of honour that no one should be charged for either food or shelter when attending these communions.[1]

The event began with preachings on Thursday, and concluded with sermons on Monday, the ministers whose parishes were involved coming to share in the duties. Sermons were preached both in the church and in the open air. The ministers in succession went out into the 'tent', an out-door pulpit covered with a roof, and walled at the back and sides. The people sat around on the turf or heather, the crowds varying with the popularity of the preacher, and were greatly moved by the sermons and prayers as the preacher's voice rose and fell in solemn cadences across the moorland or in a sheltered natural amphitheatre chosen for the services. All work came to an end, and the four days (plus two to four days more for those who travelled from afar) were given up wholly to the solemn occasion, with sermons, prayers, and psalms from early morning till late at night.

On Sunday the sacrament was celebrated in the church, with the people coming to the holy table in relays of from thirty to one hundred and fifty (according to the size of the table, church, and congregation), and addresses were given and prayers said at each table served. The service began commonly at nine in the morning, and usually continued far into the evening till darkness fell. Meanwhile, outside the church, other sermons were being preached, prayers said, psalms sung, and services of preparation and thanksgiving held.

People, with great awe and solemnity, received communion sitting at the table. In both form and kind, the elements used varied in different parts of the country, as

---

[1] The dislocation of life and work caused by these frequent festivals during the busiest farming season of the year can perhaps hardly be imagined, and it was this that led to their decline. Grey Graham gives much detail concerning these events, and quotes an estimate of the cost to agriculture as being something near £230,000 a year, an astronomical figure in those days (op. cit., pp. 313, 161).

they had done since the Reformation. In some places leavened bread was used, and in others a special kind of shortbread or unleavened bread; and the bread might be either in slices, passed and broken by each communicant, or diced as in Aberdeenshire. The wine used was normally claret, sometimes sack; and in some places water was added.

All concluded on the Monday with services of thanksgiving.

Of necessity this sketch omits much interesting detail, and the variety of pattern and local custom, but enough has perhaps been said to convey something of the august importance and centrality of what transpired, and the humility, devotion, and reverence with which our forefathers approached this holy and solemn feast.

A good deal more detail is supplied by Grey Graham, and one cannot forbear to quote one of his vivid paragraphs:

The services were not seldom deeply impressive and picturesque when held in the open air, especially when the Tables were laid on trestles on the grass. There were farmers and ploughmen in their clean but coarse homespun hodden gray and blue bonnets, the women in their white toys and the woollen plaids of scarlet or green drawn over their heads, in side groups the old lairds in their homespun cloth and sober dress, the young lairds in their laced three-corner hats, gay-coloured gilt-braided coats and jack-boots, and beside them ladies in their bright scarlet silken plaids, which, as a traveller in 1726 said, made a Scots church like a 'parterre of flowers'. The minister clad in his bob-wig, blue or gray coat and cravat, spoke in that sing-song which rose in curious cadence in the air. Even the long drawn-out psalm tunes, although broken by each line being read or sung out in turn, rose plaintive and sweet from the throng of voices; and the prayers, with their earnest, weeping pleading, came forth in a stillness broken only by sudden sighs and ejaculations, or the sharp cry of the curlew in the heather, and the song of the lark overhead.[1]

Later, he reminds us that 'it was a terrible calamity on the "great occasion" when the weather was bad, and the wind and pelting rain came on; for there was little shelter from the elements for the pilgrim multitudes; there were no woods to take refuge in, the narrow kirk could not cover them; and there must have originated rheumatism, ague, consumption, as well as an untold amount of bodily discomfort from "gospel solemnities"'. He then quotes a scene described by Mr. Thomas Boston in his *Memoirs*:[2]

On Saturday there was some thunder before we went out; between 2 and 3, when I began my sermon it returned and went to a great pitch. Upon the back of the second and third clap, I said to the people, 'The God of glory thundereth, He will give his people strength and bless them with peace'; so I went on undisturbed, the fire now and then flashing in my eyes. The people sat decently and gravely without any disturbance more than the drawing of their cloaks about them as in the case of rain. In the time of prayer after sermon the thunder went to a prodigious height, that I could not miss the imagination of being struck down in a moment, but through grace was kept undisturbed in my work.

'The picture of the minister of Ettrick', adds Grey Graham,'—himself safe from rain in his wooden tent— placidly giving two sermons, besides prayers, a psalm, and tokens, while utterly unprotected the congregation were flashed on by lightning, deafened by thunder, and threatened with a deluge of rain, is highly impressive'.[3] Impressive it is, indeed; impressive, with all its curiousness,

[1] op. cit., p. 308.   [2] p. 100 (written in 1776).
[3] op. cit., pp. 311-12.

as containing something great and holy, which in that form we shall not see again.

A word must now be said about a spectacular aspect of Scottish worship which has long faded from the scene, but endured for some 200 years after the Reformation as a constant feature: the reproof, punishment, confession, and absolution of penitents. Properly this may be said to belong to discipline, one of the 'marks' of the true Church as the Reformers taught; but in a study of worship some notice must be taken of it, since after the Reformation in Scotland it was exercised not in private, as before and at the present day (though little now remains of it), but publicly, 'in the face of the congregation', on Sunday mornings. Between 1653 and 1660 while Scotland was an occupied country, Cromwell's officers and soldiers sometimes interfered and released penitents from the jougs, but this was an exception.

The jougs and branks—by no means peculiar to Scotland—were usually fixed to the wall near the church-door, and were liberally used for the punishment of offenders. But they were not the only penalties exacted. For example, we read that in Glasgow on 18 December 1594, 'the Session enact that punishment for a single fornication is 8 days in the Steeple, one day on the Cock-stool, one day at the Pillar. A cart to be made to cart harlots through the Town; appoints a pulley to be made on the Bridge, whereby adulterers may be ducked in the Clyde; appoints the jugs and branks to be fixed up in some notable place for the punishment of flyters [scolders]'. In 1635, 'The Session appoints persons to the Correction House, both men and women, and appoints them to be whipt every day during the Session's will'. On 24 April 1645, 'Discord between man and wife first admonished;

if they continue, before the congregation; if they continue, to stand before the kirk-door between the second and third bell with a paper on their brow, and make their repentance in sackcloth at the pillar [repentance stool or pillory]'. These examples are chosen at random; kirk-session records everywhere abound in such enactments.

Under presbytery and episcopacy the disciplinary system pursued its relentless way, practically unchanged till the middle of the eighteenth century, when it was very gradually dropped. It disappeared in the end partly because a growing democratic and prosperously secular society refused gradually but resolutely to tolerate it longer; partly because the Moderates disliked what, though originally intended to be a ministry of reconciliation, had from the beginning, and certainly after 1648, (when a new Act tightened its administration), increasingly become an ecclesiastical tyranny, and would not support it; and partly because the increase of dissent made its application uneven and difficult. It was not, however, a tyranny of the ministry but also of the laity, exercised chiefly by kirk-sessions of which the minister was the moderator and mouthpiece. After the mid-eighteenth century, discipline began to be tempered by greater charity, and gradually, first in the cities and burghs, it came to be exercised in private. But it was by no means abandoned till almost within living memory; and the records of my own parish, for example, show that certain sexual lapses in particular were dealt with by the kirk-session, privately, until twenty years ago.[1]

[1] There is abundance of detail upon the exercise of discipline in kirk-session records (and also in old Presbytery records), large numbers of which are available for the research student in the Tolbooth library of records, Edinburgh, and many have been edited and privately printed through the generosity of the late Lord Bute, and are in the principal libraries, such as the National Library of Scotland. The subject in general is treated in an essay by Dr. Edgar in Story's *Church of Scotland*, v, pp.

After the Reformation, private and priestly confession and discipline were replaced by discipline exercised by the courts of the Church, and it was an unbelievably exacting tyranny (now to a large extent forgotten both by our historians and people), designed remorselessly to scrutinize and dictate moral behaviour down to the most minute detail, with the threat of excommunication (which during this period carried heavy consequences) to enforce control and punishment. This is not the place to treat of the system itself; we are concerned only with its effects seen and experienced at public worship.

Though sins and scandals might be voluntarily confessed, in fact they seldom were; and the usual process was by 'delation', that is by information of a scandal or offence being laid before the kirk-session by an elder or some other person. For example in Glasgow on 6 July 1649, 'The Session intimate that any who knows any point of witchcraft or sorcery against any person in this burgh, shall delate the same to some of the ministers or magistrates'; the kirk-session minutes throughout the country make sorry reading in the treatment of 'witches'. On 1 July 1652, we find this all too typical enactment: 'The Session appointed a clandestine committee to go about searching for persons who sell milk on the Sabbath; the committee to be four elders, and they to get 2d. a week each of them from the treasurer.'

This meant that the offences treated were always external, and the sins of the heart—pride, bigotry, malice, &c.—were not exposed; and the whole system was built up on informing and spying upon one's neighbour. As

429-556, and in his *Old Church Life in Scotland,* but his treatment is superficial; a good deal of amusing and often pathetic and even tragic incident is also to be found in Grey Graham. The best, and most recent, study is Dr. Ivo M. Clark's *History of Church Discipline in Scotland,* though for a full understanding kirk-session records must also be read to be believed, and to show the system at work; and other details may also be gleaned from diaries and journals over these years.

Dr. Ivo Clark says, 'If the compulsory confession of the Roman Church was condemned, there was something even worse in this compulsory witnessing of the faults of others'.[1] But he reminds us also that privy censures go back at least to Charlemagne, and were obviously not unknown in the early Church. Thus an Act (xvii) of 1694 could enjoin presbyteries in this to 'conform to the ancient practice of this Church'. It was, nevertheless, a grievously mischievous and poisonous system sustained by spying and informing by petty autocrats and malicious neighbours.

As, then, every minute point of morals or failure in religion was sought out by or brought to the notice of kirk-sessions, and often was taken beyond them to presbyteries and higher courts—non-attendance at worship, breaking of the Sabbath, heresy, profanity, error, sexual offences, witchcraft, mixed dancing, drunkenness, brawling, lying, cheating, stealing, scolding, and all of these rebuked and punished publicly before the congregation —there were plenty of offenders, and their reproof and 'satisfaction' provided a constantly recurring and grimly fascinating spectacle at public worship.

The assembling people as they entered the church would see these guilty sinners who had perhaps been carted in ignominy through the town beforehand standing in sackcloth at the church-door, or affixed to the jougs or other instruments of humiliation, or in earlier times standing it might be bare-legged in a tub of cold water. There they remained usually until just before sermon, then they were brought in to the pillory or repentance stool, where if the scandal was grave they might be required to appear for from six to twenty-six Sundays in succession. In 1648 (Sess. 38) an Act of Assembly following earlier precedents fixed penalties ranging from three

[1] op. cit., p. 130.

to twenty-six Sundays of 'public profession of repentance', and for oft-repeated and more heinous offences up to thirty-nine or even fifty-two Sundays. Other penalties were exacted in addition to these as the occasion demanded (and frequently, as a substitute for them, though this did not fall within the Act); these substitutes usually took the form of stated fines, which were the chief source of income to the kirk-session for the care of the poor of the parish for whom they were then responsible. And as we should expect, scandals sometimes arose out of differing treatment for the poor and the well-to-do, for the well-to-do by paying a fine could often escape the other consequences, while a poor man because of his poverty had no alternative.[1] But that is so in our courts of justice today, and must always obtain when any system of fines exists in lieu of other punishment; and kirk-sessions, because of their responsibilities for the poor, could not easily do without the income from the fines. Thus, a bad system was made worse. The 'Form of Process' of 1707 did not alter the effect of the Act of 1648.

Nor are we to be misled by the name 'repentance stool' into supposing that it was a minor article of furniture set somewhere below the pulpit, though such was often to be found for lesser offenders. The repentance stool was normally a large raised and railed platform, sometimes of two heights or grades to suit the alleged heinousness

[1] Sometimes the fines were substitutes for punishment of other kinds, as in Glasgow, 16 August 1587, 'The Session appoints that in all time coming, these fines be exacted: That servant women for single fornication by 20 lbs [i.e. £ Scots, each equalling about 1s. sterling] for her relief from Cross and Steeple. The man servant 30 lbs or else be put in prison 8 days on bread and water, thereafter to be put in the jugs. As for richer sorts of servants, to be exacted at the arbitriment of the kirk. This act not to extend to honest men's sons and daughters; but they to be punished as the kirk shall prescribe'. Sometimes they were levied in addition to other punishments, as at Tyninghame where there was never a penalty inflicted without a fine; and to undergo the penalty did not remit the fine, which was always added to the poor's box, and where no respect was shown of persons, but justice meted out with a scrupulously even hand.

of the offence, but usually of pulpit or gallery height. There stood the penitents in sackcloth, often several of them, throughout the sermon in full view of an interested congregation, afterwards to be each publicly admonished by the minister, who seldom failed to make the most of the occasion both within and without the sermon. David Allan's well-known painting, 'The Stool of Repentance', in both its versions,[1] depicts what was a familiar scene in Scotland up to a century and a half ago. These public rebukes were a source of both amusement and terror to those who were not the victims, as was evident from their smirks and anxiety, their whispers and nudges, and their often ill-concealed dismay; and it introduced an atmosphere of tremulous expectancy into what otherwise must frequently have been heavy and dull. The ordeal for the victims—except the most shameless and hardened, of which there were not a few—was a terrible one, and many rather than face it fled the country, committed suicide, or murdered their illegitimate children.[2]

At the end of their discipline, the penitents were after confession granted absolution according to the form drawn up in the 1567 'Order of Excommunication and Public Repentance', revised in 1568, printed by Lekprevik in 1569, and ordered 'to be universally within this realm observed'. The formula of absolution was as follows:

In the name and authority of Jesus Christ, I, minister of his blessed Evangel, with consent of the whole ministry of the Church, absolve thee, N., from the sentence of excommunication, from the sin by thee committed, and from all censures laid against thee for the same before, according to thy repentance; and pronounce thy sin to be loosed in heaven,

[1] The water-colour drawing is in the possession of the National Gallery, and the oil-painting in Lord Stair's collection. It is reproduced inter alia in Millar Patrick's *Four Centuries of Scottish Psalmody*, opposite p. 144.

[2] Grey Graham, op. cit., p. 323, gives some figures of these scandalous and distressing facts.

and thee to be received again to the society of Jesus Christ, to his body the Church, to participation of his sacraments, and, finally, to the fruition of all his benefits; in the name of the Father, the Son, and the holy Spirit. Amen.[1]

From these words the minister was not to vary; Sprott[2] says, 'The rubrics give very little latitude to the Minister; one of the reasons for its preparation was, that "every Church and Minister may have assurance that they agree with others in proceeding". Subsequent Acts of Assembly also enjoin that "the order prescribed shall be observed in all points", and any notices we have on the subject go to show that it was closely adhered to.' When the sin was not so heinous as to require excommunication, the procedure though public was less severe, and the form of absolution given was as follows:

If thou unfeignedly repent thy former iniquity, and believe in the Lord Jesus, then I, in his name, pronounce and affirm that thy sins are forgiven, not only on earth, but also in heaven, according to the promises annexed with the preaching of his word, and to the power put in the ministry of his Church.[3]

This formula was generally adhered to as long as the Book of Common Order continued in use; and even

[1] Sprott, *Book of Common Order*, p. 171; the whole text of these orders concerned with discipline, public repentance, excommunication, and absolution is reprinted by Sprott, op. cit., pp. 31-72, and the number of pages indicates that it was a considerable and fearsome process, even in its simplest form; they well repay study, for this is an aspect of Reformed worship conveniently forgotten by most people today.

[2] op. cit., pp. xlix-l.

[3] Sprott, op. cit., p. 54; for use of absolution at public worship, and early texts of Reformed Churches, see my *Genevan Service-Book*, p. 97, n. 4. Sometimes, also a general absolution appears to have been given, usually in preparation for the communion, as e.g. in Henderson's (1638) *Sermons, Prayers, and Pulpit Addresses*, ed. Martin, p. 9, where he concludes his Lecture on Deut. 28 with these words, 'and therefore I remit, etc.'. This suggests the use of a familiar formula, but it is not possible exactly to determine what it was; it is clear, however, that it was a definite absolution.

after it ceased, this or something similar in content was used as long as public discipline was practised.

The offenders first appeared before the kirk-session, where they were 'sharply' examined 'what fear and terror they have of God's judgements, what hatred of sin, and dolour for the same, and what sense and feeling they have of God's mercies', and, if ignorant, were instructed. Then after sermon on the Sunday appointed for their absolution they were given a lengthy exhortation, their sin specifically mentioned; prayer was then offered at some length for a due sense of sin, and that true repentance of heart might follow, and a better life. A second, more specific address was made to the penitents, one by one, and each was bidden to kneel down and make his confession; and if 'confounded with shame' or unable to speak, the minister confessed for them, each giving his assent. The people were thereafter addressed by the minister, and warned against falling into sin; a prayer of thanksgiving for the mercy of God was offered; and the penitent, having promised obedience to the discipline of the Church, was absolved with the formula above. 'Then', reads the rubric, 'shall the Elders and Deacons, with Ministers (if any be), in the name of the whole Church, take the reconciled brother by the hand, and embrace him, in sign of full reconciliation'. This form occupies eight pages in Sprott's text, and the whole action could hardly be discharged in less than twenty minutes, and must often have taken much longer. It was no light ordeal.

Among Anderson of Dumbarton's private papers I find preserved the public rebukes and remission which he gave to two flagrant adulterers taken at a communion in April 1706; and the procedure followed was similar to that described above, except that the words used were no longer prescribed. Anderson was then in his thirties, and was normally a merciful man however outspoken in some of his pamphlets; but the addresses given left nothing to the imagination.

To the woman, Janet Chalmers, who was thirty years or so older than the youth involved he refused absolution at this time: 'It will require more than ordinary charity to believe you either ingenuous or sincere, for I know you to be one of the most notorious hypocrites on the face of the earth this day'; and he was specially incensed against her because she evidently had had the temerity to 'quote David for a patron' of her adultery; apparently she was a woman who could give as good as she was given, and was not greatly intimidated by her trial. Anderson was therefore determined to break her down into repentance, but it would appear without conspicuous success. He goes on for several hundred words, and concludes, 'Repent therefore of this wickedness if perhaps it may be forgiven thee, for I perceive thou art yet in the gall of bitterness and bond of iniquity'.

Earlier he had referred to an event he had witnessed, which is an interesting commentary on the times:

I remember indeed about twelve years ago I saw the head of an adultress chopt off upon a scaffold, and when the people saw that her hairs were gray and lymed it increased their indignation and lessened their pity, but after all she was a saint in comparison with you for besides that she was much younger, though her accomplice in wickedness who suffered death at the same time with her was married, yet she herself wanted a husband, and therein your wickedness is above hers. . . .

And he went on,

Mother of harlots and a whore yourself and a bawd to others, I dare confidently aver that in all Sodom there was not a worse house than what you kept, fornication or adultery in every corner of it, and at the same time what could tempt you to such a sin; nothing surely but such an unquenchable lust as nothing but the unquenchable fire of hell can resemble.

In all, his addresses to her and to the people occupy four pages of typed foolscap, when copied, and Anderson was no doubt typical of his day in his whole treatment of this case.

The youth, Duncan Campbell, he addressed sternly, but with compassion: 'You compear there to be rebuked for the sin of adultery with Janet Chalmers. Your sin is truly so heinous in itself, and attended with such black circumstances, that I want words to express myself on this occasion.' He then refers to the Law given upon Sinai, 'with smoke and fire and sound of trumpet which was so dreadful that even Moses said, I exceedingly fear and quake, and the people were next to dying with fear. . . . How fearful will that day be when the Lord Jesus shall be revealed from heaven in flaming fire to take vengeance on them that know not God, nor obey the gospell, when not one mountain only, but the whole world shall be on fire; whither will ye then run for a hiding place?' And so on, dealing next particularly with his sin, and calling him to repentance; and finally, 'Now confession being the first evidence of repentance, get down upon your knees and confess your sin in the sight of God, implore his mercy and beg the prayers of his people for you that you may be received as a returning prodigal'.

After the youth had made his confession, Anderson says,

As I desire to believe you are ingenuous, so I earnestly beg of God the Father of Mercies that he would have mercy upon you and vouchsafe a pardon. I have no desire to imbitter your spirit with harsh words, but encline rather to restore you in a spirit of meekness, but for your safety I must tell you that it will require more than an ordinary repentance to restore you to the favour of God; your repentance must bear some proportion to your offence if you expect it should be effectual to any good purpose, and a holy after life will be the only solid evidence of such a repentance. Cry earnestly to God for grace and strength to resist after tentations. Beware of casting yourself in the way of them. Remove thy way far from her and come not nigh the doors of her house, for her house is the way of hell going down to the chambers of death. I remitt you for absolving the profession of your repentance to the Congregation where the sin was committed.

What does this last sentence mean? The writing is clear, and that is what Anderson undoubtedly wrote. I conjecture that 'upon' or 'after' had inadvertently been omitted (Anderson was not able to review his unpublished papers before his death) before 'the profession &c.'; the meaning would then be, 'I remit you for absolution after the profession of your repentance before the congregation where the sin was committed'. I have quoted at some length, though in fact from only a small part of the document, to give a typical picture of the words used.

In Anderson's time, the procedure was, after sermon, to rebuke the penitent (who stood in the stool of repentance throughout the sermon) at length and in detail concerning the nature and consequences of his sin. After this, he was required to kneel down and confess his sin aloud before the congregation; he was then exhorted to a true repentance and a good life, and absolution was pronounced; and the minister concluded by addressing the people in the light of what they had witnessed, applying to them the dangers of falling into the sin under review, and exhorting them to resist temptation and lead a good life following the commandments of God. It was a terrifying experience for a sensitive person, for much must have passed in comment outside the church as well as inside; and even for the most hardened it must have been a subduing ordeal. Such then was one considerable aspect of public worship in Scotland for more than two centuries after the Reformation.

VI

The Renascence of Worship

WE pass now to the period from about 1750 onwards. Charity of judgement and tolerance had increased among all classes, agriculture was beginning to be scientifically studied and practised, bringing with it not only wealth to the landowners but a vast betterment in the conditions of life to the farmer and farm-servant; and the improved roads and means of travel bound the country together into a growing unity. Education reached a higher standard and became more generally available, the towns grew and prospered industrially, culture and grace of living became more general among the lairds and upper classes, music was practised and enjoyed, and a school of landscape and portrait painters arose with Alexander Nasmyth as a pioneer. Acceleration in all this began to show itself about the middle of the century: manners became more gentle, taste began to be more widely cultivated, and among the clergy reading and education walked in broader paths.

· 'Never did the Church', writes Grey Graham,[1] 'hold so high a place as in 1750-70 in attainments, position, and esteem. In the General Assemblies met the men most conspicuous for worth and ability, both lay and clerical; and in the debates, ministers of distinguished talents, and elders who were the most accomplished and brilliant Scotsmen, took their parts. In the absence of

[1] op. cit., pp. 359-61.

a Scots Parliament, the Assembly was looked upon and used as a nursery for orators and politicians, and there was to be found almost as good speaking as in the House of Commons.' In contrast, the ministers at the beginning of the century, with their wailing rasping voices inherited from the 'antediluvians' (i.e., the pre-Restoration men), were, speaking generally, though 'thoroughly respectable, even eminently respected, pious and faithful', also 'narrow, uncouth, and superstitious . . . and whether they were sprung from poorer classes, farmers, or "merchants" or lairds, there was less difference in manners between ranks in the country then'.

Never did the clergy in Scotland sink in social esteem and position like the common clergy in England in the beginning of the eighteenth century. . . . The Ministers described in the memorable *Tour of the Hebrides*—living far remote from towns and libraries, in inaccessible regions of the Highlands, appear as men of good sense and breeding, vigour and learning, so as even to extort growling regard from the anti-presbyterian lexicographer. But nowhere is higher praise given from a competent source than in 1772 by Pennant,[1] the traveller who knew them so well: 'They are much changed from the enthusiastic, furious, illiterate teachers of old times and have taken up the mild method of persuasion instead of the cruel discipline of corporal punishment. They are the most decent and consistent in their conduct of any class of

[1] *Tour in Scotland*, i, p. 173. We find two interesting contemporary opinions of Pennant in Boswell's *Life of Johnson*: 'Books of travels having been mentioned', writes Boswell, 'Johnson praised Pennant very highly. "He's a *Whig* Sir; *a sad dog* (smiling . . .). But he's the best traveller I ever read; he observes more things than anyone else does." ' Boswell did not agree: 'I could not help thinking that this was too high praise of a writer who had traversed a wide extent of country in such haste, that he could put together only curt frittered fragments of his own, and afterwards procured supplemental intelligence from parochial ministers, and others not the best qualified or most impartial narrators, whose ungenerous prejudice against the house of Stuart glares in misrepresentation; and who it should seem from a desire of ingratiating himself with the Scotch, has flattered . . . so inordinately and with so little discrimination, that the judicious and candid among them must be disgusted.'

men of their order. Science flourishes almost universally among them, and their discourse is not less improving than the table they entertain strangers at is decent and hospitable', and 'they preserve with a narrow income a dignity too often lost among their brethren south of the Tweed'.

These were the Moderates—is it not time we had a good word to say for them?—to whom Scotland in truth owes so much; nor is this to detract from the great contribution made by evangelicals and seceders during the same period; with more patience and generosity of mind each might have understood the other's worth. Not only did the seceding ministers and the evangelicals within the Church contribute by their zeal and ardour, always an essential leaven in the full catholic faith, but also by their direct influence towards a richer worship; evangelicals of the Relief Church were the first to introduce hymns, and some brought back into use the Lord's Prayer and the doxology, appreciating also the value of historic prayers, 'the divinely approved petitions of saints'.[1] As M'Crie has said, 'No man of fairness will fail to allow that the record of the Seceders all through the period of decadence was a noble one, a record of splendid service to the cause of Christ and the historic Church of Scotland'.[2] This is a just tribute, biased only in its gratuitous reference to decadence.

Lord Cockburn, whose *Memorials* are not always strictly accurate, also makes a typical Whiggish generalization about this period, and supports the Whig myth of decadence, so long accepted by historians. 'The old historical glory had faded; and under the insignificance of repose, it was chiefly a lower description of men who were tempted to enlist in the ecclesiastical service. The humbleness of their living and the cheapness of their education

[1] United Associate Synod's *Testimony*, 1827. [2] op. cit., p. 308.

vulgarized them still more. Indeed, learning and refine-
ment ceased to be expected; and with too few exceptions,
vegetating in the manse, and the formal performance of
parochial duties, came to be the ultimate object of clerical
ambition. The descent of the Scotch clergy throughout
the last half of the eighteenth century was steady and
marked', he writes. But when he goes on to particularize
by specific illustration we find that he is speaking not of
the last half of the eighteenth century but of the early
nineteenth century, and of that period he does speak
somewhat more accurately. 'Take the case of Edinburgh',
he says, 'to which the best clergymen may be supposed
to have been allured [another doubtful generalization]':

About the year 1790 we had Blair, Henry the historian,
Hardy the eloquent Professor of Church History, Principal
Robertson, Dr. Erskine, and Sir Harry Moncrieff; all literary
and agreeable gentlemen, the delight of all society. But
twenty years showed the change that was proceeding. Sir
Harry alone remained, and not one other person had arisen
to fill up the vacancies. I do not recollect a single work of
any importance, which any one of our established clergy contributed during this time to learning, or to science, or even
to theology; and in Edinburgh at least, but I believe everywhere, they had fallen almost entirely out of good lay society.

Had all this been compensated by higher professional
eminence, it might have been said, that what this world had
lost the Church had gained. But at this period, this could
not be said with even a pretence of truth. It was the reverse.
Until Chalmers arose the theology and eloquence seemed to
be worn out. . . . A new Presbyterian revolution, however,
was approaching, which brought out new men, and new
dangers, and new popularity, with a necessary elevation of
those who shone in it. But about this time the old thing
was dead.[1]

That was the picture as Lord Cockburn saw it, but it

[1] *Memorials of His Time*, ed. W. Forbes Gray, pp. 140-1.

is by no means a whole picture; Grey Graham's is less partial, and helps us better to understand what was happening at the beginning of the renascence of worship, for it must properly be dated from the last part of the eighteenth century. Save that the reader's service had disappeared—certainly not an advantage, for it meant a decline in the reading of Holy Scripture in the churches —the changes in structure were slight. But a new sobriety, orderliness, and seemly dignity began to be seen in the services of the Church, and the prayers possessed a new directness of speech—fewer colloquialisms appeared in them, there was less histrionic 'wrestling', weeping, and smiling; it was beginning to be seen that speech and language addressed to the Most High God differed from that addressed merely to man; and if prayers were usually still long according to our standards, they began to gain in dignity and brevity as compared with what was general earlier in the century.[1]

Here, for example, is a consecration prayer used at an ordination at Kirkgunzeon in the Presbytery of Dumfries on 4 August 1747. It is taken from a MS. collection of sermons which I have in my possession,[2] but the writer is not known. It serves, however, to illustrate a style of prayer used by a country minister at this time; and it is also of passing interest to note that he had carefully prepared and written his prayer for this occasion:

FATHER of mercies, God of all grace and consolation, with gratefull minds we adore thy goodness that shines with a conspicuous lustre and dazzling glory in the face of Jesus our divine Saviour, whom thou hast been pleased to send into the world for the redemption of guilty mankind, and for restoring them to a primitive, holy, and happy state. We thank and praise thee with our whole hearts for all the

---

[1] See my *The B.C.P. and the Worship of the Non-Anglican Churches.*
[2] The gift of Dr. Francis Eeles.

advantages we enjoy by the Gospel, for the clear discovery of thy will and of our duty, for the gracious promises of thy apostles, and the encouraging prospect of a glorious reward to animate our obedience. We bless thee for the wise instruction of religious ordinances and for the gifts and graces of thy holy Spirit which thou bestowest upon men to qualify them for dispensing these ordinances unto thy people that they may be trained up for the noble and exalted enjoyment of a future state.

Do thou, O most Mercifull Father, pour down a double portion of thy holy Spirit upon this thy servant whom we now in thy name and by thine authority set apart and consecrate to the holy ministry in this congregation. Give him grace to fulfill the work of his ministry in all things, to feed the Church of God committed to his charge with so much care and fidelity as that both he and his flock may be saved in the day of the Lord Jesus when he comes to call us to an account for our stewardship. Adorn his mind with all those virtues that will make him shine as a light in the world: And may he be the happy mean, in thy providence, of bringing this people from darkness to light, from the power of Satan unto God. All which we humbly implore for the sake of Jesus. Amen.[1]

The increase of pews, replacing the former stools and benches, helped to create a greater attitude of reverence and good manners;[2] formerly it had been common for

[1] See Church Service Society *Annual*, 1951, pp. 29-31, for the service in full.

[2] See p. 100 supra. Till well past the middle of the eighteenth century manners in church were very free, and this can be seen at a glance in Allan's painting referred to earlier, for Allan was not 'Hogarthian' but a genuine recorder of the life of his period. The records too give information to support this, and the Glasgow record of a century earlier throws light on behaviour in church in the seventeenth and much of the eighteenth centuries: 25 March 1665, 'The same day the beddelship of the Laigh Kirk in Trongate is conferred upon and given to James Smith, merchand; and he is not onlie to be careful anent the ringing of belles, but also he is to walk throw the kirk in time of divyne service, with ane whyt staff in his hand, as wont to be of old, for the crubbing of bairns and others, that maks disturbance in the kirk and for impeiding all abuses therein.' See also Henderson, *Sermons*, p. 8.

people to move about and talk during service. The interesting spectacle of the penitents disappeared. People now everywhere reverently stood during prayer. This was not yet a liturgical awakening, but there was an increased reverence and propriety in worship. Further, the quickened sense of worship in England and numerous suggested reforms of the Book of Common Prayer were not without their effect upon Scottish ministers who read the works of their authors. This is clearly apparent in such publications as *The Scotch Minister's Assistant*, first published at Inverness in 1802, and running into several editions during the next twenty years,[1] and such works as *Holy Communion*,[2] containing strong arguments for a return to the primitive and early Reformed practice of weekly communion, which came from the pen of Scots ministers abroad and were published and widely read in this country.

Between 1760 and 1830 Scotland experienced a period of considerable intellectual development, and produced in the realms of art, letters, and science many figures of international repute. This was accompanied by vastly improved agricultural methods and the expanding Industrial Revolution, both of which contributed to improved living standards and a greatly increased population. The last factor brought with it the need for new churches as well as the replacement by more adequate structures of diminutive and decayed rural churches of medieval origin.[3] While the loss of some of the more interesting of those pre-Reformation buildings is to be regretted, the new churches were in the main architecturally superior to those they superseded. One of the most gracious

---

[1] Title later changed to *Forms of Prayer for use in Church of Scotland*.

[2] J. M. Mason, *Letters on Frequent Communion*, 1803. See Sprott in *Euchologion* edition, 1905, for a further list of these early Scottish books on worship.

[3] These were followed by the neo-Gothic churches which continued to be erected into Edwardian times. While there were some of real merit, on the whole the results in Scotland do not give cause for pride.

features of this Georgian period is the developed Renaissance architecture of the many country houses and urban buildings which were produced by architects and craftsmen of skill for clients of taste. As far as means permitted, the new churches were built in this elegant style, and there is little doubt that many of them are not unworthy contributions to our architectural history.[1]

At last, the real merit is now being recognized of many of these heritors' churches of this period, so often sneered at in the past as poor in materials and of a 'bastard classical design'; and many of the defects formerly criticized are seen to be owing to the neglect or 'renovations' of succeeding generations rather than to the conception and construction of the builders. The beautiful windows paned with clear glass, have been denuded of their graceful astragals and filled with frosted glass, or a repulsive greenish pebbled glass so widely favoured seventy-five years or so ago; the exteriors have been allowed to get dirty or dull, or have even been washed with a yellowish brown, in the niggardly interest of economy; and the interiors have been stencilled and genteelly coloured and patterned. A coat of whitewash on the exteriors, clean pastel paint on the interiors, and the restoration of the windows would transform many of these churches into places of light and beauty, for in nearly all of them the proportions are fair and pleasant, if they were but allowed to be apparent. Also, they were admirably suited to the mode of worship of the day, with the pulpit central to the long side of the rectangle or at the cross of the T, and the communion table running the full length of the main axis; and if now they require some remodelling to meet the changes in our manner of worship and of ministering holy communion, this should

[1] Leishman, op. cit., *v*, pp. 415-16, in common with many other writers, greatly overstates the merit of the medieval churches and underrates the new. Cf. Geo. Hay, op. cit.

never be done without the most careful study and the advice of an architect skilled in work of that period, and with a competent knowledge of the modern requirements of our rite.

Extremely detrimental to the serene simplicity of these churches have been the many commercial installations in the late nineteenth and early twentieth centuries of pipe-organs with their aggressive and intrusive pipes blatantly occupying a central place in the sanctuary instead of being modestly housed in the west gallery or at the west end where they properly and traditionally belong. 'Renovations', too, were carried out in this period—they called them 'restorations'—upon many of our ancient churches; so often they were destructive, and apart from preserving the fabric, deplorable. Nor have we yet learned to be cautious, scholarly, and painstaking in the renovation of our churches; for many nowadays are still being done in the best Edwardian Anglican manner, with narrow passages, high mean steps,[1] ill-proportioned holy tables and cluttered sanctuaries and chancels. Sentimental love of the House of God as the place where His honour dwelleth is not enough; it must also be informed love, born and expressed of knowledge.

When we turn to examine psalmody, we find just after the turn of the half century a new movement led by Channon who came to Aberdeenshire in 1753;[2] and in due course it spread over the country bringing dignity and beauty in simplicity to the Church's praise. As we have seen, the preposterous practice of 'lining' had become universal in Scotland during and after the Cromwellian

[1] Scots architects to a large extent, for example, still have an extraordinary propensity for 6-in. risers in steps, and seem unable to distinguish between domestic and ecclesiastical architecture in this matter, and so in their renovations and even in new churches contribute resolutely to the disfigurement of our sanctuaries. See my *Concerning Worship* for specific guidance.

[2] Millar Patrick, op. cit., p. 149.

period, and psalmody was dismal beyond description. Twelve common-metre tunes formed the canon of music in Scottish praise for nearly a century from 1666, when the first collection of tunes for the new psalter was published in Aberdeen;[1] and it is doubtful if all twelve were ever or long operative; in fact, the number of tunes used in most parishes seems not to have been more than two or three. No organs were permitted; the precentor led the praise. And most precentors were more remarkable for their idiosyncrasies than for their knowledge and skill. We cannot linger here over the old stories which abound in memoirs of the time, but many have been collected by Dr. Millar Patrick in his account of Scottish metrical psalmody.

New horrors, however, were yet to be invented by precentor and people alike. Not content with the simple tune, which in any event most could not sing, they fell to embellishing it with grace notes of their own devising, often invented on the spot, each singer owning allegiance to his own fancies alone. Thus, together with lining and gracing, the cacophony created is mercifully unimaginable to modern ears despite the strain to which they are still sometimes put. The tune was unrecognizable, though many precentors protected themselves from this charge by displaying the name of the tune, boldly if rudely printed on cardboard set in front of their desk. 'What tune are they at?' asked a late arrival at a church in Berwickshire of his neighbour. 'I no ken', was the answer; 'I'm at the Auld Hundert.' And the remarks of an Italian music master once passing the open door of the Tron Church, Edinburgh, when song was in progress, expressed the utmost bewilderment.

But the musical revolution after 1753 led by the English foot-soldier, Thomas Channon, under the patronage

[1] ibid., p. 111.

of Sir Archibald Grant of Monymusk gradually changed all that. The great movement began in Aberdeenshire, and not in city but in country parishes. It consisted in the dropping of 'lining',[1] and the training of choirs, together with these simple reforms: choosing tunes, old and new, with discrimination; teaching them 'truly and plain', without quavering or any kind of affectation; observing 'the proper time'; and introducing the use of harmony.

It is not, of course, to be thought that this movement succeeded all at once; there was great opposition for a long period, and even secessions occurred over it. But it did grow and increase, and a new standard was established, which spread rapidly throughout the country, so that its effect was widespread within ten years. Choir lofts now began to be built in churches at the west end to accommodate the choir, some holding as many as 120 persons. In other churches, the elders were thrust out of their traditional place in benches round the pulpit, and the singers installed there.

This musical renascence was accompanied by the publication of large numbers of tune books with which psalmody was enriched, or debauched, according to the varying quality of what was supplied. But a renascence had begun, which as the years passed yielded rich fruit, and sent musicians examining into the treasuries of the past, out of which a corpus of notable psalm and hymn

---

[1] The General Assembly in 1746 recommended 'the ancient practice of singing without reading the line', but it was slow of adoption—e.g., 1757, St. Machar's, Aberdeen; 1766 in one church in Edinburgh—and it lingered on in many places for a century longer, and in remote Highland parishes till within living memory, if indeed it has yet wholly disappeared. It is, however, merely just and true to say that in spite of the disadvantages of lining, psalmody in Highland churches often attained a singular beauty, and the pathos and triumph of worship, born of the Celtic genius for music, a genius that could not be fettered and which was able to transform the very obstacles of lining and gracing into vehicles of loveliness and devotion creating an effect not unlike the early responsorial psalmody.

tunes has been built up, comprising some of the most dignified music of Christendom.

The first extraneous additions to the metrical psalter were the Scriptural paraphrases which appeared in 1745; but they were not finally accepted in use till forty years later, and were never officially adopted by the Church of Scotland.[1] At first they met with violent opposition, and some secessions occurred when they were introduced. Now they are regarded as precious and singular to our tradition, as indeed they are; but their introduction was the occasion of many and sometimes acrimonious differences. The chanting of prose psalms was first suggested by Dr. James Beattie,[2] but nearly a century passed before this became a feature of Scottish worship in some of the city and burgh parish churches.

The restoration of organs and organ accompaniment aroused for some time heated opposition, often resulting in scenes of mob-rule, when the newly-installed organs were removed and publicly burnt or destroyed after service. But the protests failed, and organs quickly became universal. The pioneers were Dr. J. Marshall Lang[3] in the newly-opened church at Anderston, Glasgow, in 1860, and a few months later Dr. Robert Lee of Old Greyfriars, Edinburgh.

Some years earlier than this, when Marshall Lang was minister at East Church, Aberdeen, and still a youth in his twenties, he had preached an eloquent sermon on the

[1] The standard work on the paraphrases, a very complicated subject, is D. J. Maclagan's *The Scottish Paraphrases*; see also Millar Patrick, op. cit., and M'Crie, op. cit., pp. 282 sqq.

[2] In *A Letter to the Revd. Hugh Blair D.D., on the Improvement of Psalmody*, printed in 1778 but not published until 1829.

[3] Two of Dr. Marshall Lang's sons became in later years, one the Archbishop of Canterbury, and the other Moderator of the General Assembly. On his introduction of the organ, see his letter in J. Kerr's *Renascence of Worship* (Lee Lecture, 1905), pp. 88-90. Previously, there had been an abortive attempt to introduce an organ in St. Andrew's Church, Glasgow, in 1807; it is now preserved in the People's Palace.

M

value of kneeling for prayer and standing for singing, and, not a little to his surprise, after sermon the congregation, deeply impressed, spontaneously adopted these attitudes; but his neighbour, the minister of the West Church, carried the matter of this heinous innovation to the presbytery, which solemnly ordered the congregation of the East Church to revert to its former custom. Being young, and not desirous of setting his youthful judgement against that of a court of the Church, Marshall Lang acquiesced.[1]

The first organs were either harmoniums or American organs,[2] but pipe-organs followed swiftly and became a formidable feature in Scottish churches.

After the Oxford Movement some country parsons in England going up to the great churches which consisted of nave, quire, and chancel discovered the singers in the quires, and coming back to their parish churches brought their singers into the chancels to imitate as nearly as possible what seemed to be the approved thing; and, Scottish ministers, going south and admiring, followed this unfortunate example in the late Victorian and Edwardian period, and, oddly, are doing so still in some places. As a result, many of our sanctuaries are now crowded with stalls, chairs, organs, and singers many of whom mistake the office of chorister for that of concert singer, and with an invincible determination worthy of a better cause suppose that they must face the people when they sing, and will go to any lengths to do so. Thus so many of our sanctuaries, instead of being spacious places of dignity where the holy table stands in austere simplicity, are

---

[1] We soon find the movement spreading rapidly; e.g. 'Mr. Usher moved that steps now be taken to alter the usual forms of worship in the church in so far that the congregation should be invited to kneel at prayer and stand at singing. . . . The Session unanimously agreed' (Kirk-Session Minutes, Canongate, 5 December 1864).

[2] Dr. Marshall Lang's was a pipe-organ, Dr. Lee's a harmonium to begin with. In the Canongate a harmonium was introduced in June 1874.

cluttered, crowded, and restless; and, as if this were not bad enough worse still has been devised, for the irreverent and banal indignity is not unknown of organ consoles being made to serve as communion tables.

However, distressing as were the designs of most of the new organs and deplorable as were usually the places selected in the churches for their erection, they did bring a new enrichment and orderliness to Scottish praise. Soon after this, hymns were introduced into the Church of Scotland;[1] and to these were added anthems and prose psalms. But to comment in detail upon the renascence in congregational and choral music, begun 200 years ago, and receiving new and splendid impetus in the last seventy-five years, would require a volume in itself. The movement has been fostered by the Church through its Aids to Devotion Committee, and within the former United Free Church through its Psalmody Committee; and it is still active, the music of the Church reaching an increasingly richer and more diverse expression under a skilled and devoted group of musicians and organists to whom a sufficiently high tribute can hardly be paid.

Turning now to other aspects of worship,[2] we have

---

[1] The *Scottish Hymnal* for use in the Church of Scotland was published in 1870, other editions following rapidly. The Relief Church's Hymnal had been published in 1794, that of the Secession Church in 1852, and that of the Free Church followed in 1882. Hymns from other collections began to be introduced in Scottish parish churches at least as early as the 1860s, as for example, 'It was agreed to bring the subject of the use of hymns sanctioned by the General Assembly for the public worship of Canongate Church prominently before the congregation in order to induce them to purchase copies with the view of their general introduction into the church service' (Kirk-Session Minutes, 5 October 1863); and in the next year we read, 'It was unam. agreed to raise a sum by subscription for the support of an efficient band, the members of which would be required to officiate regularly at both diets of worship under Mr Gardiner the precentor', who 'was held responsible for having an efficient choir for the church' (Minutes, 8 February 1864). 'Band' and 'choir' are synonymous.

[2] We are not to forget the witness of the novelists from this period onwards, interestingly collected and displayed by Dr. A. L. Drummond in his *Churches in English Fiction*, pp. 202-32.

observed that there was a quietly discernible improvement in the general conduct of worship from 1750 onwards: prayers became shorter (though still long by our standards), more chastely phrased, and less histrionically offered. There was, however, a long established tendency to use an unwritten liturgy, and to mistake it for extemporary prayer. Dean Ramsay, a regular attender at Banchory Church from 1815-22, remarked upon the minister's prayer there being 'rigidly and precisely the same as much as any liturgy could be'.[1] A letter of Archbishop Benson's dated 1848 says: 'Last Sunday we went to Kirk [at Crathie]. . . . Within there is no Communion Table, no font, nothing Christian and holy looking. . . . The service . . . was as like as possible to what I remember of the Independent system—no [prose] Psalm, no first and second lessons, no Glory to the Father, no Lord's Prayer even. From the minister's manner it was clear that every Sunday there was exactly the same kind of prayer a little varied in expression, and Mr. W. assured me that it is so—that in fact the objections against a liturgy as formal are nil, and to the specious name of heart-prayer is sacrificed all the beauty of worship.'[2] And A. K. H. Boyd writes a little gruffly in Fraser's Magazine in 1857: 'If you hear a decent, commonplace, rather stupid Scotch minister pray, every sentence would fall quite familiarly on your ear if you were a Scotsman. It is the regular old thing, only the component parts a little shuffled.'

Nevertheless, there was an improvement upon former days. Sermons also were more carefully prepared and

---

[1] *Presbyterian Liturgics*, Edinburgh, 1858.

[2] *Life*, i, p. 47. We are not to suppose that the archbishop was without bias, but he is not the only one to have remarked upon the 'unwritten liturgy', and many will still remember it; there is no doubt that for the most part ministers' prayers though extemporary varied little from Sunday to Sunday and the old familiar expressions and catenas from the psalms and Holy Scripture recurred with obvious frequency. Archbishop Benson's description is not applicable to Crathie now.

delivered; the introduction of the read sermon stirred much controversy but there can be little doubt that it greatly improved preaching, and reduced rant and cant; and in the hands of such masters as Edward Irving and Thomas Chalmers, and later, Alexander Whyte and John Caird and many others, who would venture to declare it to be ineffective? Nevertheless, the particular changes in general order were slight until after the disruption in 1843: the changes consisted rather in an improvement of the parts. This was no doubt chiefly because controversy in the Church of Scotland centred upon other matters, culminating in the disruption.

In 1824, an innovation was made, however, in the manner of communicating in St. John's Church, Glasgow, by which the elders distributed the sacred elements to the people in their pews, the backs of which were covered with white linen houseling cloths, instead of the people coming forward to the tables as formerly. This innovation was in fact borrowed from old English Puritan practice, transmitted through the Congregationalists and Anglicans of the day. It was the commonly accepted method of administration in the Congregationalist Churches, but was known also and used within the Church of England at this time for, as J. C. Bowmer has remarked, 'in the nineteenth century at St. Mary's Oxford the pews were covered with "houseling cloths" and the communicants had the elements brought to them. Dr. Pusey, of all people, used to administer in this way at Christ Church, Oxford, as late as 1856, and it was also the custom at Trinity College, Cambridge, fifteen years later.'[1] There had been debates on the subject at the Westminster Assembly in 1644, the Scots refusing to accept the method. Likewise, in 1825 it was debated in

[1] *The Sacrament of the Lord's Supper in Early Methodism*, p. 9; and F. Bond, *The Chancel of English Churches*, pp. 122-3.

the General Assembly, and condemned: to sit 'at or around a Communion Table or Tables' was declared to be 'the law and immemorial practice of the Church of Scotland'. But general opinion especially among the laity favoured the practice, and it gradually spread—quickly in the large congregations. The service was reduced in length by many hours; for, instead of successive tables, one normally served, with perhaps a second in the afternoon; thus the practice is now all but universal in large and small congregations alike. The process of change occupied more than one hundred years.

The *Statistical Account* of Campsie gives an example of what the service was generally throughout the country about the end of the eighteenth century:

The Sacrament is given once in the year [parishes still combined, though not on the previous scale—now usually only two or three parishes uniting]: three discourses on the fast day, two on Sunday, two on Monday; the action sermon in the church, and the evening sermon, besides preaching in the tent. People have complained that the tent preaching was prejudicial. I am inclined to believe the contrary from experience: first, on account of its bringing a considerable collection for the poor; and secondly it accustoms a number of people to meet together in a decent, cheerful, and respectable manner.[1]

Such a passage [writes Leishman] gives no conception of the length of the Sunday service. Not less than two hours passed before the minister left the pulpit to head the procession of elders bearing the Communion elements and vessels to the Table. Each successive company of communicants not only received the sacrament, but listened to an address on the ordinance, both before and after, so that nearly half an

[1] Tent preaching was not always accompanied by such respectability, and had in fact given rise in some places to grave scandal (see, e.g., Grey Graham, op. cit., pp. 311-13, and p. 152 supra). The reasons the minister of Campsie gives in favour of the practice are themselves mirrors of the age.

hour passed between their taking their places and rising again. The last of these services was followed by an address from the minister of the parish to the whole body of communicants, and that by a sermon of thanksgiving by another preacher. In large congregations, requiring twelve or fifteen table services, a circuit of the clock was sometimes nearly completed before the worship was. Of this series of services, the last stage was the 'perlicuing' (*perlego*) before the benediction was spoken on Monday. The minister of the parish summed up, as well as his aptitude and memory allowed, all the discourses which the people had heard, the preachers listening with varied feelings as their productions were mangled or mended.[1]

Here also we may include John Wesley's description of a communion service he attended with misgivings at St. Cuthbert's parish church, Edinburgh, on 16 June 1764; for it gives a clear if unflattering picture by an outside observer of the form generally followed in the century before Chalmers's innovation of carrying communion to the people in their pews.

Sat. 16. We had a ready passage at Kinghorn, and in the evening I preached at Calton Hill to a very large congregation, but a still larger assembled at seven on Sunday morning in the High School yard. Being afterwards informed that the Lord's Supper was to be administered in the West Kirk I knew not what to do; but at length I judged it best to embrace the opportunity, though I did not admire the manner of administration. After the usual morning service, the minister enumerated several sorts of sinners, whom he forbade to approach. Two long tables were set on the sides of one aisle, covered with table-cloths. On each side of them a bench was placed for the people. Each table held four or five and thirty. Three ministers sat at the top, behind a cross table, one of whom made a long exhortation, closed with the words of our Lord; and then, breaking the bread, gave it to him who sat on each side of him. A piece of bread was then given to him who sat on each side of him. He broke off a little

[1] op. cit., v, p. 410.

piece, and gave the bread to the next; and so it went on, the deacons [elders?] giving more when wanted. A cup was then given to the first person on each bench, and so by one to another. The minister continued his exhortation all the time they were receiving; then four verses of the twenty-second Psalm [vv. 25-28?, with the words, 'The meek shall eat, and shall be filled'], while new persons sat down at the table. A second minister then prayed, consecrated, and exhorted. I was informed the service usually lasted till five in the evening. How much more simple, as well as more solemn, is the service of the Church of England![1]

The general form of ministration was the same everywhere, but there were local differences, many of them dating back to the Reformation, e.g., along the Solway unleavened bread [not wafers] was specially made; in Aberdeenshire, the mixed chalice was traditional. There were also later differences, e.g., as between Lifters and Anti-lifters.

The number of parishes combining for communion services began to be reduced from 1750 onwards, for agriculture and work suffered too greatly. The fast days disappeared more slowly, and it is not till 1887 that we find them abandoned in Edinburgh. In the kirk-session minutes of the Canongate,[2] it is recorded, for example, that the presbytery and town council had conferred on the question of public holidays, it having been found for some time past that the fast days no longer served their religious purpose but were kept merely as holidays. The kirk-sessions of all the city churches were consulted, and it was generally agreed that the old fast days should be abandoned, and other times suitable for holidays be in due course fixed by the town council.

Earlier, the Oxford Movement, and the liturgical movement which followed it, had made themselves felt in

[1] N. Carnock (ed.), *Journal of the Rev. John Wesley*, V, pp. 77-78.
[2] 7 October 1886; 4 November 1886, &c.

Scotland, and many within the Church began to examine anew the origins and doctrines of Christian worship, the Church, and the holy ministry. Thus we find in 1849 a committee appointed by the General Assembly to prepare forms of service for those, at home or abroad, who were without a minister; and the second book of prayers issued by the Church[1] since the Book of Common Order appeared in 1858 entitled *Prayers for Social and Family Worship*. This may seem but a slight advance, yet it denoted a remarkable change of attitude and climate; in this book the prose psalter was used, the Lord's Prayer, and Scripture lessons. Two years before this, the General Assembly had specifically enjoined the clergy to read lessons from both Testaments at the Sunday Services, and generally to conform more closely to the Directory. Nor was this injunction unnecessary; as late as 1857 such expressions as this were commonly heard: 'The reading of the Bible in church is a mere waste of time—we can read our Bibles at home.' 'The mutilated form of the Protesters', as Dr. Sprott says, 'had come to be regarded as embodying that purity of worship which the Reformers restored, and for which the Covenanters fought and died.' The next year, in 1859, an Aids to Devotion Committee was appointed by the General Assembly under the convenership of Professor Crawford, and it continues an influential and active committee of the General Assembly still.

The *Liturgy and Divine Offices* of the Catholic Apostolic Church also influenced considerably the development of the worship in the Church of Scotland, and particularly in the ordering of the Lord's Supper.[2] This influence

[1] The booklet for family worship mentioned by the minister at Tyninghame was the first; see p. 108 supra.

[2] See Dr. H. C. Whitley's thesis on Edward Irving, in the Edinburgh University library. Irving, a founder of the Catholic Apostolic Church, was at one time an assistant to Dr. Thomas Chalmers, though his attitude to ecclesiastical reform differed greatly from Chalmers's.

came chiefly through Dr. John Maclead of Govan, and it is interesting to compare his *Communion Office* (published anonymously and undated) with the Catholic Apostolic liturgy.

Things were moving more or less quietly forward, when they were first disturbed, as we have seen, by the young minister of East St. Nicholas Aberdeen, Mr. Marshall Lang; then later the storm broke on Dr. Robert Lee at Old Greyfriars Edinburgh, who had dared not only to install a harmonium but to institute new liturgical services boldly printed in a book, the people standing to sing and kneeling to pray. His service-book, *Prayers for Public Worship*, was a work of his own genius, and exhibited no basic knowledge of liturgics (indeed, he was impatient of reference to the historic liturgies), but its intention was good, and the style of the prayers terse, concrete, direct, and Scriptural.

All this excited much controversy, which forced into closer association men concerned to improve worship, and out of it the Church Service Society originated on 31 January 1865. With many of the most eminent and scholarly clergy and teachers as its leaders, it grew quickly and steadily until more than a third of the clergy were members.[1] The Society was accorded a liturgical leadership by the Church, and the leadership was scholarly, conservative, and wise. A small group of scholars wrote books and pamphlets expounding the origins and history of Scottish worship—Sprott, Wotherspoon, Leishman, Cooper, Story, and others—while the smaller Scottish Church Society studied doctrine and made a massive contribution to our understanding of Church, ministry, and sacraments. The Church Service Society also issued services for special occasions and Christian festivals.

Most noteworthy was *Euchologion or a Book of Common*

[1] See J. Kerr, op. cit., for a detailed account.

Order[1] published in 1867, the chief compilers of which were G. W. Sprott of North Berwick, R. H. Story of Roseneath (later, Principal of Glasgow University), and Principal Tulloch of Edinburgh University. *Euchologion* met a long-felt need, and ran into a large number of successive editions for fifty years and more. It made a distinctive and brilliant contribution to the renascence of Scottish worship, drawing in its prayers from many sources, ancient and modern, and adding its own creative work.

The early editions of *Euchologion* set forth an order of service for ordinary Sunday use very similar to that commonly prevalent but with some elaboration, and the whole and the parts of the service more clearly ordered. What was then general use we know from a report made to the General Assembly in 1864 by Dr. Hill, who at the previous Assembly had been appointed convener of a special committee to consider worship. He reported that 'almost universally the order is as follows: Praise, Prayer, Reading of Scripture, Praise, Prayers, Lecture or Sermon,[2] Prayer, Praise, Benediction; that the use of the Lord's Prayer was general, but that some used it only occasionally and some not at all; that in Old Greyfriars the prayers were printed, and that a harmonium had been in use for nearly a twelvemonth'. He concluded the report by saying that while 'the Church may claim the

---

[1] The first edition was supplied with a good preface, excellent notes, and mention of sources; and the 7th edition, 1905, contains an introduction and notes (not wholly accurate, but still of great value) by Dr. Sprott; see also Barkley, op. cit., vi, pp. 1 sqq. On the successive editions, see M'Millan's article, in Church Service Society's *Annual*, 1936-7, pp. 24-33. The Form for the Celebration of Holy Communion was used by the General Assembly from 1890 to 1923, an indication of the approbation with which the book was received by the Church. A book of *Daily Offices* was published by the Society in 1893.

[2] As the reading of the Scriptures began to find a place during the nineteenth century in the Sunday worship either the lecture or the sermon was dropped. Formerly both had existed side by side.

power to interfere with ministers and congregations adopting a closer observance of the Directory than custom demands or sanctions', legislative measures were both 'unnecessary and inexpedient'.

The order recommended by *Euchologion* was first confined to the prayers, but a Table of Lessons from the Old and New Testaments was provided 'for each Lord's Day' to cover a period of two years, for both morning and evening services.[1] This lectionary attempted to include the chief passages of the Old Testament, most of the Epistles, and the whole of the Gospels, but the lessons were perforce too long. Its influence, however, was very marked, and a new emphasis began to be laid upon the reading of the Holy Scripture in the worship of the Scottish Church. The prayers were three in number: the first prayer consisting of 'Introductory Collect, Confession of Sin, Prayer for Pardon and Peace, Supplications, and Concluding Collect'; the second, 'Thanksgiving, and Prayer for Illumination before Sermon'; the third, 'Collect after Sermon, General Intercession, and Concluding Prayer'. It was recommended that 'the Lord's Prayer may conclude either the First or Second Prayer'. To use the Lord's Prayer in either of these positions was contrary to Scottish use both before and after the Reformation, and we see here the influence of Anglican morning and evening prayer making itself felt, for the positions recommended for the Lord's Prayer are derived directly from the Prayer Book. The influence of the Prayer Book was to become more dominant still as time passed.

Euchologion contained also orders for the ministration of Holy Baptism, for the Celebration of the Lord's Supper, and for many other offices. The Order for the Celebration

---

[1] Evening services began to be introduced about the middle of the nineteenth century in place of the afternoon service. The change first took place in city parishes, but made its way slowly and was not general till the twentieth century.

of the Lord's Supper or Holy Communion alone con-
cerns us here. It was preceded by a brief historical
explanation, indicating what was common to the experience of the Church beginning with New Testament times;
then the order, with prayers, was set down, having one
distinct peculiarity an innovation of the times, in that the
principal intercessions followed communion. It was influenced in much by the rite of the Catholic Apostolic
Church, but is by no means derived from that rite, and
it follows the Directory closely.

The service took its usual course till after the sermon;
at which point there was introduced an exhortation of
moderate length, compiled chiefly from the Book of
Common Order, with some paragraphs from the Book
of Common Prayer, and with the ancient τὰ ἅγια τοῖς
ἁγίοις, translated 'Holy things which are for holy persons'. The offertory followed, taking the form usually of
the singing of Paraphrase 35 ('Twas on that night), during which the alms might be collected, and the minister
and elders bring in the elements in solemn procession to
the communion table; and the communicants take their
places. The minister then salutes the people with the
grace, reads the words of institution (1 Corinthians
11.23-26), and this is followed by a brief address upon
the meaning of holy communion, concluding in Calvin's
manner with the *Sursum Corda*.

The Apostles' Creed follows in the form of a prayer,
and a prayer of access, which begins with a confession of
sins and prayer for pardon and concludes with the prayer
of the veil.

Now the prayer of consecration begins, 'It is very
meet, . . .', with thanksgiving for creation modelled upon
Eastern liturgies and relating the fall and redemption of
man, for providence, for redemption, the sending of the
Holy Spirit, for the sacraments and ordinances of the

Church, the communion of saints, and hope of everlasting life, concluding with the *Sanctus*, 'Holy, Holy, Holy, Lord God of Sabaoth, &c.', and the *Benedictus qui venit*, 'Blessed is He that cometh', with Hosannas. Thereafter follows the epiclesis or invocation, and the Lord's Prayer. Then comes the fraction and delivery, somewhat confused and intermingled, and the communion; after communion metrical Psalm 103 is sung.

A brief exhortation to thankfulness is then given by the minister, and the post-communion prayer of thanksgiving and self-oblation, closely modelled on the Prayer Book, follows, and after it the great intercession, and thanksgiving for the Church Triumphant. Then the *Nunc dimittis* is sung in the metrical version, and the minister pronounces the benediction.

This order is not wholly satisfactory, particularly in the consecration prayer, which is influenced too much by the fashion of the times, but it served as a model valuable in itself, and helped to foster the study of the historical liturgies and Reformed worship. It was not greatly changed in succeeding editions, except that the introductory historical exposition (never of course part of the service) was unfortunately dropped. In the fifth edition (1884), the Nicene Creed was given preference to the Apostles' Creed in the communion service.

But in 1890, in the sixth edition, against the advice of its best liturgical scholars, a group within the Church Service Society managed to bring about a revision by which the order of morning worship was made to conform more closely with Anglican matins, and indeed with the prevalent Victorian manner of saying matins. This was more pronounced in the seventh edition (1896) of which Dr. Sprott says, 'It was resolved to change the order of public worship as follows: the Lord's Prayer to be said both by minister and congregation at the close of the first prayer [a custom then popular in the Anglican Church, when often the Lord's Prayer was omitted after the little litany at Morning Prayer], and the intercessions and thanksgiving to precede the sermon [also derived from common practice at Anglican Morning Prayer]. From this resolution there were dissents, the chief reason, besides the departure from Primitive and Reformed usage, being that the order of the communion which is the normal service of the Church should be followed as closely as possible at other times. The old order, however, was printed as an alternative (p. 176).'[1]

This brought certain enrichments: the use in a few places of responsive prayers, and a wider use of the prose psalms to Anglican chants. But it was an unfortunate and amateur departure from the traditional Scottish structure of worship, and in principle and content the loss was greater far than the gain, for matins began to usurp the eucharist as the traditional norm of Scottish worship, and that diversive influence has not yet wholly passed.

Mention must be made also of the St. Giles' Book of Common Order, written and compiled by Dr. Cameron Lees and in use in the cathedral from 1884 to 1926. Dr. Cameron Lees 'was one of those far-seeing men who in the latter half of last century turned the minds of many people in Scotland towards a worthier conception of common worship than was commonly in vogue among the clergy at that time. He saw that the old High Kirk of St. Giles, steeped as it was in centuries of Scottish devotion, deserved to have a liturgy at once dignified and real. This was necessary not only for the Sunday services, but also for the orderly conduct of daily service. So in 1884, a year after the cathedral was restored to its proper unity mainly by the generosity of William

[1] Sprott, in *Euchologion*, ed. 1905, p. xxi.

Chambers, there was published a *Book of Common Order for Sunday and Week-day Services* . . . to be used until such time as "another formulary be set forth by the proper authority".[1] Thus there came into being a service-book used every day in this historic church; and at communion the order in *Euchologion* was followed. The book was revised and shortened later by the reverent and skilful pen of Dr. Wallace Williamson. The liturgical revival has been still active under the ministry of Dr. Chas. H. Warr, and for many years now there has been a weekly celebration of holy communion there; and in an increasing number of Scottish churches holy communion is celebrated at least monthly.

Although the General Assembly's Committee on Aids to Devotion gave guidance in worship over many years, and issued services for special occasions with increasing frequency, it was not till 1923 that an official service-book was issued for voluntary use not merely with approval but 'by authority' of the General Assembly. It was entitled *Prayers for Divine Service*, based on *Euchologion*, the Book of Common Prayer, and other service-books, and drew material from the ancient liturgies. The prayers were brief and direct, and the whole of a high order, but marred by its dependence on matins for the Sunday morning worship. Nor was it improved by an enforced revision appearing a few years later. It did, however, set a fine standard of devotion and public prayer, and very rapidly established itself in wide use.

Meantime, liturgical societies had been formed in both the United Presbyterian and Free Churches, uniting with these Churches in 1900.[2] In 1928 the United Free Church

---

[1] C. T. Thornton, in Church Service Society *Annual*, 1953-4.

[2] See Church Service Society *Annual*, 1930-31, pp. 79 sqq., for an account by Dr. Millar Patrick of the Church Worship Association of the United Free Church; this Association united with the Church Service Society in 1930. The tributary societies of the Church Worship Association were:

published with the approval of the General Assembly, its service-book, entitled The Book of Common Order 1928.

In 1929, the Churches united, and a first action of the General Assembly was to appoint a Committee on Public Worship and Aids to Devotion, combining the Committees of the two Churches. A few years later, it was charged with the task of preparing a service-book to comprehend the full Scottish and Reformed tradition as a branch of the Catholic Church. The result was the Book of Common Order 1940, which was issued also by authority of the General Assembly. It is now the authoritative standard of the Church of Scotland, but its use is not compulsory. It is, however, in wide and steadily growing use, and, presented to every divinity student in his first year, it provides a basis of instruction in the universities.

Of outstanding excellence in this book are the orders for the ministration of the sacraments and other ordinances, and in particular the first Form and Order for the Celebration of the Lord's Supper or Holy Communion, which represents a long tradition brought to a high perfection, indigenously Scottish and Reformed, and essentially Catholic. In its dignity of action, centrality of content, and felicity of expression, it provides a vehicle of worship entitling it to a place among the great rites of Christendom, and is rapidly being recognized as such. Indeed, its influence in many other communions is notable, not only in the daughter churches, but even at Geneva itself where, translated into French, it is a rite used in Calvin's Church of St. Peter.

the Devotional Service Association (U.P. Church) formed in 1883, which published a service-book entitled *Presbyterian Forms of Service* (1891, 1892, 1899); and the Public Worship Association (Free Church), formed in 1891, which published *A New Directory for Public Worship* (1898), which contained prayers as well as directions. The Church Worship Association, formed in 1901, published a valuable *Anthology of Prayers* (1907, 1908) and a *Directory and Forms for Public Worship* (1909).

In addition to this book, the Assembly's Committee has also issued, the first edition in 1935 and a revised edition in 1952, *Prayers for the Christian Year*, which contains services for the principal festivals of the Church's year; the *Ordinal and Service Book for Use in the Church Courts* (undated) in 1931, with a revised edition in 1954; and *Forms of Prayer for Use at Sea*, 1936, is now under revision. It also issues many services for special occasions, and has published a long series of informative pamphlets of which large numbers are in frequent demand.[1]

The Church Service Society still continues its work, having a membership of some 700 ministers and laymen, including branches in the daughter Churches of the Commonwealth. It publishes an *Annual* each year, containing papers and articles on the various aspects of Christian worship.

Thus the renascence of worship leavens the life of the Church, and the movement happily is largely devoid of controversy and division, both in itself and in the Church. Holy communion is celebrated more frequently, as we have seen, throughout a large portion of the Church, and weekly communion is not unknown. The old Reformed basic order is in many places restored, together with such significant and evangelical ceremonial as standing for the reading of the holy Gospel; and the lectionary has been revised to include the central truths of Holy Scripture. For the last fifty years or more new churches have been built on the traditional rectangular or cruciform ground plan, with central communion table and side-pulpit, and some significant architecture has resulted, not least in new church-extension churches; and large numbers of older churches have been effectively renovated to accord

---

[1] The various service-books and hymnals of the Church of Scotland are published by the Oxford University Press; and other publications of the Aids to Devotion Committee are obtainable through the Church of Scotland Publications Department, 121 George Street, Edinburgh.

with basic principles of worship, and a growing sense of responsibility is evident. Freedom of worship, which has become a treasured tradition in the Scottish Church, still prevails, and the services therefore often differ considerably throughout the Church in their content and order. If much remains to be accomplished, none has been untouched by the liturgical movement, which from the beginning has been concerned to preserve, and, where necessary, to re-establish what is best and deepest in the tradition of the Scottish Church, remaining steadfast to the great evangelical principles of the Reformation, yet remembering that the Church of Scotland is, as she has always asserted herself to be, a part of the holy Catholic Church. The liturgical movement in the Church of Scotland has, on the whole, been directed by a loyalty to basic principles securely founded in the central tradition of the Church, steadied by a sense of history and propriety, and perpetually aware that it is God revealed in Jesus Christ as Father, Son, and Holy Ghost, to whom all worship and obedience is due, and that 'man's chief end is to glorify God, and to enjoy Him for ever'.

INDEX